The Book of Tea

by
Kakuzo Okakura

Edited and Introduced by
EVERETT F. BLEILER

Dover Publications, Inc.
New York

This Dover edition, first published in 1964, is an
unabridged and unaltered republication of the work
originally published by Fox, Duffield and Company
in 1906. A new Introduction and Afterword have
been specially written for this edition by Everett F.
Bleiler.

International Standard Book Number

ISBN-13: 978-0-486-20070-5
ISBN-10: 0-486-20070-1

Library of Congress Catalog Card Number: 63-17913

Manufactured in the United States by LSC Communications
20070137   2017
www.doverpublications.com

CONTENTS

IV. The Tea-Room 30

The tea-room does not pretend to be other than a mere cottage—The simplicity and purism of the tea-room—Symbolism in the construction of the tea-room—The system of its decoration—A sanctuary from the vexations of the outer world

V. Art Appreciation 42

Sympathetic communion of minds necessary for art appreciation—The secret understanding between the master and ourselves—The value of suggestion—Art is of value only to the extent that it speaks to us—No real feeling in much of the apparent enthusiasm to-day —Confusion of art with archaeology—We are destroying art in destroying the beautiful in life

VI. Flowers 50

Flowers our constant friends—The Master of Flowers —The waste of Flowers among Western communities— The art of floriculture in the East—The Tea-Masters and the Cult of Flowers—The Art of Flower Arrangement—The adoration of the Flower for its own sake— The Flower-Masters—Two main branches of the schools of Flower Arrangement, the Formalistic and the Naturalesque

VII. Tea-Masters 61

Real appreciation of art only possible to those who make of it a living influence—Contributions of the Tea-Masters to art—Their influence on the conduct of life —The Last Tea of Rikyu

Afterword 67

INTRODUCTION

During the second half of the nineteenth century, in the reign of the Emperor Meiji, Japan set out on her remarkable program of modernization. Her rulers saw clearly that if Japan was to survive as a nation, she must be able to match in power the White Disaster which had entered with Commodore Perry. The government invited scholars of all sorts, including military experts, from the chief nations of the West, and founded new universities at which they could teach. The most promising young Japanese graduates of these universities were then sent to Europe and America to study the new sciences at first hand. The program sounded easy at first, for the young men learned quickly. But difficulties arose: modernization, it became apparent, meant much more than just discarding the old Chinese mystical physics and studying Baron Helmholtz or Lord Kelvin, or permitting foreign embassies to open in Tokyo, or driving a railroad bed through ancient cedar groves. It gradually became clear that modernization meant the destruction of an entire way of life.

Most Japanese accepted the new ideas loyally. Ancient feudal families donned trousers, learned to sit upon chairs, and turned to mercantile enterprise, which had hitherto been considered degrading. They tried to think like Westerners, and even tried to eat beef (forbidden by Buddhism)—though they often gagged as they ate.

Not all Japanese, however, were willing to accept the government's program. Many thought that the price was too high, and that too much of value was being lost; others resisted change for selfish reasons. The first opposition was direct and violent, in the 1860's, when military feudalists as medieval as the knights in Froissart rebelled and were finally crushed by military force. A generation later, however, in the same era which produced Vivekananda and Tagore in India, there emerged a new, more subtle generation of protest against Westernization. It is probably significant that while the reaction in India was religious and political, in Japan it was moral and aesthetic.

Among the most important of these late nineteenth century aestheticians who tried to shelter the morning-glory during the transplant by keeping some of the ancient mould around its roots was Kakuzo Okakura, the author of that minor English classic *The Book of Tea.*

The Okakura family had been samurai in Fukui Province until the middle of the nineteenth century, when Kakuzo Okakura's father set himself up as a silk-merchant and moved to Yokohama, where Kakuzo was born in 1862. The family prospered, and Okakura was sent to the new Tokyo Imperial University, then an English-language institution, where he took a Master of Arts in 1880, with honors in philosophy and English literature. He already had a good grounding in Chinese.

One of the cardinal concepts of Oriental thought, from even before the time of Confucius, has been the belief that alternating, diametrically opposed forces govern the universe, like day and night. They are called the yang and the yin in Chinese. One is dark and female; the other is bright and male. Each prevails for a time, but within it, like a seed or germ, rests the other force, which will eventually emerge and rule. Such was the case with young Okakura, for in the very heart of Westernization, at the Tokyo Imperial University, he learned to value his own culture by studying under the remarkable Ernest Fenollosa. Fenollosa, a Harvard-educated New Englander, had come to Japan to teach philosophy and political science, but had surrendered with delight to the traditional arts and culture of Japan. More than any other man Fenollosa halted the trend toward Westernization in the arts and awakened new understanding for the native heritage of Japan.

It is now difficult for us to realize how much of old Japan had been cast aside in the desire for new ways. The public schools were obsessed with teaching European perspective and chiaroscuro, and the older Japanese techniques were either derided or ignored. This had gone so far that even the native ink brush, which had been perfected over centuries for painting and writing, had been banned from the schools, and its place taken by the clumsy Western oil brush. And the treasures of ancient Japanese art were not only no longer understood; they were often viewed with some embarrassment. Old families, in need of cash for the new monetary economy, were selling heir-looms for a pittance, and there are even stories of monasteries and temples where out-of-style wooden Buddhas were converted into firewood. So much Japanese art, indeed, was bought at fantastically low prices by understanding Americans like Fenollosa and Edward Morse and W. S. Bigelow that it is still necessary for Japanese to come to America to see much of their national heritage.

Fenollosa's enthusiasm and dynamism converted Okakura, as it had others, and the two worked closely together, Okakura serving as Fenollosa's interpreter in lectures and on trips. They began to receive encouragement, and with a government directive in hand authorizing them to make an inventory of religious art, they explored the repositories of ancient relics, gathering and preserving such treasures as were still in existence. Van Wyck Brooks, in his recent *Fenollosa and His Circle*, conveys very well the enthusiastic delight with which Okakura and Fenollosa uncovered masterpiece after unsuspected masterpiece in the lumberrooms, storage chambers, and abandoned sections of the temples. Their work was not unappreciated, and when the government took a sudden swing away from the West, Fenollosa, besides being awarded assorted decorations, was given an imperial commission in 1886 to study art history and museum techniques in Europe. Okakura and another Japanese went along.

Upon their return to Japan, however, Okakura and Fenollosa drifted apart, since they apparently no longer found it possible to work together, despite mutual respect and common interests. The reasons seem to have been personal, for both men were aggressive and egotistical and capable of high emotion over questions of art. Added to this was a certain resentment as Okakura outstripped Fenollosa, who was never really at home in Oriental languages. In 1890 the energetic Fenollosa left Japan and became curator of Oriental art at the Boston Museum of Fine Arts, and Okakura, unofficial head of the conservation movement and principal of the Tokyo Art School, started his independent career.

Always controversial, perpetually embroiled in personal quarrels and palace intrigues, by 1898 Okakura had fallen badly out of favor with the government, and he resigned his official post to found a new school, the Japanese Art Institution, for the study of the arts and their philosophical premises within the Great Tradition. This was an Oriental school of the most extreme sort: there were no illusions about who was master; there were no ambiguities about its point of view. It was Asiatic, for during his maturity Okakura came to recognize that acculturation was not just a Japanese dilemma, but one that affected the other Asiatic nations as well. He came to conceive of India and China (the major sources of Asiatic civilization) as pieces with Japan of a larger, traditional culture that was diametrically opposed to the evolution-obsessed ways of the West. More and more the concept grew upon him that his mission was "protecting and restoring Asiatic modes of thought and life." In 1902 he visited Rabindranath Tagore in Bengal, and received a tumultuous welcome, for he was now a figure of Asiatic stature. India was especially prone to accept his basic point of view: "The old art of Asia is more valuable than that of any modern school, inasmuch as the process of idealism and not of imitation is the raison d'être of the art impulse."

There were difficulties, however; the government refused to support Okakura's school, and the school needed funds desperately. Okakura met the situation by gathering together a group of art objects, and sailing for America, where the market was then booming, to sell them. This was a crisis point in his life, just as had been his meeting with Fenollosa, for Okakura remained in America, having found in Boston the haven he had not been able to find in Japan.

In America Okakura renewed acquaintance with the painter John Lafarge, whom he had known when Lafarge and Henry Adams had visited Japan a few years earlier. Lafarge passed him along to Isabella S. Gardner of Boston, whose fabulous Italian Renaissance palace was becoming the center of an eclectic art movement in Boston.

"He is the most intelligent critic of art," wrote Lafarge to Mrs. Gardner, "and I might say, of everything, that I know of. His very great learning in certain ways is balanced by his perception of the uselessness of much that he knows." This was an apt introduction, for Okakura was a very learned man by both Western and Oriental standards, as well as a man who believed that knowledge should be useful.

Okakura delighted Mrs. Gardner and her associates, since he was able to convey all the glamour of the Orient together with a remarkably solid corpus of knowledge. He sold his art works for the Institute, sent his travel associates back to Japan with the money, and decided to remain in America. He lectured on the arts of the Orient, and through Mrs. Gardner's connections he addressed the International Conference of Culture and Literature at the International Exposition at St. Louis, 1904. He was heard as enthusiastically as had been Vivekananda in Chicago a few years earlier, for America was highly receptive to intelligent Orientals.

The parallel paths of Okakura and Fenollosa continued to cross and anticipate one another. Fenollosa, under circumstances that are not clear, left the Boston Museum of Fine Arts, and in 1906 Okakura became Advisor, and in 1911 Curator of Chinese and Japanese art. He was a remarkable choice, for under his direction the collections were brought to a peak of perfection, with even a colony of Japanese artisans being settled in Boston to repair and restore damaged pieces. The Oriental collections of the Boston Museum became world-famous, and it has been said that with Okakura the study of Oriental art attained its first maturity. He stressed a systematic coverage of the ranges of art (as opposed to isolated pieces), and travelled back and forth to the Orient almost seasonally to collect new pieces.

His trips to China would probably make fine novels, if half the rumors that one hears about them are true. He travelled in disguise, with a false pigtail, trusting to his mastery of Chinese to carry him through the unsettled country. He managed to obtain fabulous art treasures at a time when Chinese collectors were hiding their possessions in panic to avoid confiscation. Without these trips, it is safe to say, our American collections of Chinese art would be considerably poorer.

During this period of frantic education, collection, classification, lecturing, and travel, Okakura still managed to write profusely for American and Oriental journals. He also saw three books published during his lifetime: *The Ideals of the East* (1903), *The Awakening of Japan* (1904), and *The Book of Tea* (1906). A fourth, *The Heart of Heaven*, appeared in 1922, nine years after his death.

In 1913 he returned on his annual visit to his wife and children in Japan, and in September news of his death reached Boston. He had died of influenza in Tokyo. He was mourned in America, and is still remembered as the author of *The Book of Tea*.

ii

Until now I have spoken of Okakura only as an energy who did certain things, as a dynamism who did a great deal to change history by processes which he set in motion. What sort of man was he personally ?

This is not an easy question to answer, for he was

a strange mixture of brilliance and infantilism, penetrating vision and the most ostrich-like reaction. He was a man with a mission, and he suffered from the contradictions that often constitute missionaries. He was affable and charming to his friends, and he was also arrogant, irascible, and sharp-tongued to persons who irritated him—who were many, since he could not tolerate opposition. He had a clear vision of the dangers that faced Japanese culture at a time when "progress" was interpreted very naively in both the Occident and the Orient, and yet he also suffered greatly from cultural myopia: he was sentimentally attached to the most absurd trivialities of Japanese history, and often was unable to distinguish between the rubbish and detritus of a dead past and the weak components of a living (though submerged) tradition that deserved to be fostered. Osvald Sirén states this dichotomy with great insight when he says that "Okakura was one of those rare men in whom the intuitive sentiments, perhaps a little vague, of the Japanese, were mixed with the analytical faculties of the Occident."

Perhaps we can understand Okakura and also *The Book of Tea* if we examine Okakura as a multiplicity. First, there was Okakura the scholar. He was unquestionably a man of genius, one of the great historical scholars of the modern world. He knew the Orient as few men ever have, for he combined the sharp focus of the West with a native knowledge of Japan, Korea, China, and other lands. His knowledge of all branches of Oriental art was, for its day, unequalled, and he was almost as familiar with Indian culture as with the Far East. He was also a remarkable linguist, as can be seen in this book, which was written at white heat in English.

Okakura the messiah is second. Despite his charm

and a range of deep friendships, Okakura was basically an impatient and intolerant man with the knack of making enemies. His life-path was strewn with quarrels. Even worse, he had a remarkable gift for repartee, and he usually won verbal duels brilliantly, since he always thought immediately of the things that others wished later they had said. He was also something of an opportunist, though a peculiarly unselfish one, and there seems to be little question but that he managed to down his former associate Fenollosa. He was a violent authoritarian as a teacher, demanding absolute obedience from his followers. At times he behaved more like a lamaist abbot than a teacher of aesthetics. In protest against Westernization he designed curious robes and headdresses which he wore in his school in Japan. He often made a nuisance of himself.

Personality number three is the strangest of all. Here was a profound scholar and religio-cum-aesthetical martinet, who also wore a most tender heart upon his flowing sleeves. He could gush about kittens in letters to Mrs. Gardner. He could write English poetry that might pass for weak Swinburne. And he could also write about the fairy-tale past of Japan as if he believed in every goblin and fox-woman and slashing samurai in the whole corpus of folklore. This was Okakura the sentimentalist.

All of these personalities emerge in his work. The great scholar holds forth in learned articles. The sentimentalist runs away with much of the work posthumously published in *The Heart of Heaven*, parts of which can justly be called puerile. The visionary and messiah have too large a part in *The Ideals of the East* and *The Awakening of Japan*. The first of these two books is a clear statement of the esoteric philosophy of art later continued by such men as Coomaraswamy; the second book can be repugnant to the Western reader because of its religious awe for the supernatural claims of the Mikado, emphasis upon purity of blood, and a sympathy for the more unpleasant cultural aspects of nationalism.

The best synthesis of the many personalities of Kakuzo Okakura took place within the well-known *Book of Tea.* Here a remarkable fusion occurred among disparate elements. Okakura the scholar revealed his knowledge; Okakura the visionary and messiah pointed this knowledge with direction; Okakura the appreciator clothed it with charm. The result is one of the most delightful essay-volumes in the English language.

iii

The Book of Tea is a modern English classic, and hundreds of thousands of Americans have read it as a delightful introduction to the Japanese way of life. Okakura apparently wrote it in English, without the assistance of his English-speaking friends, and read it aloud to Mrs. Gardner's circle. The language is truly a remarkable achievement—easy, graceful, remarkably clear and precise.

Yet beneath its surface of color and charm *The Book of Tea* is very largely an apology for the conservative facet of Japan. It is an attempt to explain to the Western world, symbolically, why the Japanese feel as they do about aspects of their culture. There is no soft romanticism about it, however, as there is about the stories or essays of Lafcadio Hearn. Its flowing English and delightful allusion mask a steely hardness of thought that is as sharp and incisive as the sword of an ancient samurai.

Okakura wanted to explain the peculiar orientality of the Orient, and used tea as his symbol. In the Far East tea stands parallel with our own concept of salt; it can mean the inner essence which imparts meaning and savor to something that might otherwise be drab or tasteless. Okakura probably did not create this genre of a symbol-book, however, for as widely read a man as he must have been acquainted with parallel forms of literature. There have been many Near and Middle Eastern works in which "Life" is expressed in terms of jewels, and about the time that Okakura wrote, books were being published in Europe and America in which tobacco served as the theme of life. It seems very likely that Okakura was acquainted with Arthur Gray's *Little Tea Book*, a collection of quotations and associational material about tea, which had appeared in 1903.

Okakura worked through the uniqueness of tea. He first tells of its origin, early history, and diffusion, and then points out the eye within the symbol in Japan: the tea-ceremony, that peculiarly Japanese ceremony which is not followed elsewhere in the Orient. This tea-ceremony is a quasi-religious ceremony, performed under conditions codified centuries ago, where a group of people gather and go through rites as fantastically rigid as ever a worshiper performed for a stiff god. Time and place are determined by rules; décor of the chamber, utensils, actions, and even conversation proceed upon the most controlled path, with formulas controlling both deed and word. The host makes traditional gestures of welcome, and the guest admires the utensils in phrases as meaningless and archaic as the tea-pouring itself.

Yet the tea-ceremony, properly speaking, is not a

religious rite, since no supernaturalism is involved. It is a social sacrament. It is a bridge to the past over which the dead ancestors swarm. It involves a submission of one's self to the ways of the fathers. It means that you must do things according to the old ways.

From another point of view the tea-ceremony is quite remarkable in the study of institutions. It is one of the very few examples of an attempted ritualization and mechanization of the aesthetic impulse—the belief that an enactment of a standardized "drama" will arouse the sensations which beauty arouses. We in the West almost uniformly consider the aesthetic feeling to be an individual concern, and, no matter what theory we hold about its causes and nature and manifestations, believe that it arises spontaneously; normally, we do not even consider the possibility that it can arise from ritual *dromena* and *legomena*. Our situation is perhaps a little strange, since in our religions we have ritual on all levels, from the church ceremony which the layman attends, to the meditations of the religious athlete. Just as the Jesuit may practice the Spiritual Exercises of St. Ignatius, or the Tantrist may meditate upon the attributes of the Goddess, or the Sufi upon the Divine Attributes, the celebrant of the tea ceremony meditates and attempts, by establishing an empathy, to recapitulate an aesthetic experience.

In the West we obviously find our acceptances and negations socially structured, but nowhere except in the religious practices of the specialist do we have such a totality of predetermined response as the tea-ceremony demands. Even in ordinary religion, where gesture and word are controlled, we demand a certain sincerity, and in matters of art and beauty and delight we are even more religiously insistent upon sincerity than we are in religion. Perhaps this is because we have gone through the early nineteenth century emotional revolution, where individual feeling and honesty of emotion took precedence over mechanism and properness.

Tourist brochures showing handsome geishas pouring tea to mixed company are far from the facts of the true ceremony, especially as it was celebrated in Okakura's time. The tea is a muddy, thick, gray liquid, made by suspending a powder in water, and it is necessary to brush the scum and dregs from the top before one can drink. And little beauty is to be found in the ceremony. The utensils are often considered ugly by the Japanese themselves, and there has been considerable criticism directed at the inflated prices which enthusiasts have paid for ugly old vessels. Tea vessels and whisks and stirrers are not judged by the same standards as other Japanese art, and their value depends upon peculiar criteria. Desirability does not arise from beauty as is the case with most Japanese artifacts, nor from iconological significance, as might be expected from a cultic apparatus. Instead, their value is primarily derived from a third criterion: antiquity and personal association. They are almost part of a cult of saints, with relics. Whenever a great tea-master's bowl comes upon the market, it has tremendous financial value.

It is strange in a way that a man like Okakura, who spent most of his life in the netting of beauty and the preservation of its fragile essence, should have found the arch-symbol of Japan in the tea-ceremony. Perhaps it is an aspect of his reaction against the West. In some ways the tea-ceremony shatters the two great art theories which have pervaded Occident and Orient: it disavows individual appreciation of art for art's sake, which has been the way of the

West for several centuries; and it disavows iconology, or the ideas for which an image stood, which has been the way of India and the Far East. It sets up a third category, imitation for the sake of antiquity, imitation because this was the way of the ancestors, and the ancestors must not be questioned or doubted.

The presuppositions of *The Book of Tea* are intimately related to the basic question of what one should think about Okakura and his lifework. One possible answer is that the scales of good and bad stand even. He created and preserved beauty, and yet he also used beauty as a calculated tool for an unworthy purpose. His great book, *The Book of Tea*, has aroused Americans to sympathy with Japanese modes of thought, and yet the same ideas in the Orient (where others may have had more historical importance than did Okakura) have served as a focus for hostility to other cultures.

Perhaps, when judging Okakura, one should bear in mind the idea basic to much Asiatic religion: beings of power, like gods and demigods, have both good aspects and evil aspects, and do not fit facile categories. One must accept such a being for what he is.

E. F. BLEILER

New York
1963

I. THE CUP OF HUMANITY

Tea began as a medicine and grew into a beverage. In China, in the eighth century, it entered the realm of poetry as one of the polite amusements. The fifteenth century saw Japan ennoble it into a religion of aestheticism,—Teaism. Teaism is a cult founded on the adoration of the beautiful among the sordid facts of everyday existence. It inculcates purity and harmony, the mystery of mutual charity, the romanticism of the social order. It is essentially a worship of the Imperfect, as it is a tender attempt to accomplish something possible in this impossible thing we know as life.

The Philosophy of Tea is not mere aestheticism in the ordinary acceptance of the term, for it expresses conjointly with ethics and religion our whole point of view about man and nature. It is hygiene, for it enforces cleanliness; it is economics, for it shows comfort in simplicity rather than in the complex and costly; it is moral geometry, inasmuch as it defines our sense of proportion to the universe. It represents the true spirit of Eastern democracy by making all its votaries aristocrats in taste.

The long isolation of Japan from the rest of the world, so conducive to introspection, has been highly favourable to the development of Teaism. Our home and habits, costume and cuisine, porcelain, lacquer, painting,—our very literature,—all have been subject to its influence. No student of Japanese culture could ever ignore its presence. It has permeated the elegance of noble boudoirs, and entered the abode of the humble. Our peasants have learned to arrange flowers, our meanest labourer to offer his salutation to the rocks and waters. In our common parlance we speak of the man "with no tea" in him, when he is insusceptible to the serio-comic interests of the personal drama. Again we stigmatise the untamed aesthete who, regardless of the mundane tragedy, runs riot in the springtide of emancipated emotions, as one "with too much tea" in him.

The outsider may indeed wonder at this seeming much ado about nothing. What a tempest in a tea-cup! he will say. But when we consider how small after all the cup of human enjoyment is, how soon overflowed with tears, how easily drained to the dregs in our quenchless thirst for infinity, we shall not blame ourselves for making so much of the tea-cup. Mankind has done worse. In the worship of Bacchus, we have sacrificed too freely; and we have even transfigured the gory image of Mars. Why not consecrate ourselves to the queen of the Camelias, and revel in the warm stream of sympathy that flows from her altar ? In the liquid amber within the ivory-porcelain, the initiated may touch the sweet reticence of Confucius, the piquancy of Lao Tzŭ,[1] and the ethereal aroma of Sakyamuni[2] himself.

Those who cannot feel the littleness of great things in themselves are apt to overlook the greatness of little things in others. The average Westerner, in his sleek complacency, will see in the tea ceremony but another instance of the thousand and one oddities which constitute the quaintness and child-ishness of the East to him. He was wont to regard

Japan as barbarous while she indulged in the gentle arts of peace; he calls her civilised since she began to commit wholesale slaughter on Manchurian battle-fields. Much comment has been given lately to the Code of the Samurai,—the Art of Death which makes our soldiers exult in self-sacrifice; but scarcely any attention has been drawn to Teaism, which represents so much of our Art of Life. Fain would we remain barbarians, if our claim to civilisation were to be based on the gruesome glory of war. Fain would we await the time when due respect shall be paid to our art and ideals.

When will the West understand, or try to understand, the East? We Asiatics are often appalled by the curious web of facts and fancies which has been woven concerning us. We are pictured as living on the perfume of the lotus, if not on mice and cockroaches. It is either impotent fanaticism or else abject voluptuousness. Indian spirituality has been derided as ignorance, Chinese sobriety as stupidity, Japanese patriotism as the result of fatalism. It has been said that we are less sensible to pain and wounds on account of the callousness of our nervous organisation!

Why not amuse yourselves at our expense? Asia returns the compliment. There would be further food for merriment if you were to know all that we have imagined and written about you. All the glamour of the perspective is there, all the unconscious homage of wonder, all the silent resentment of the new and undefined. You have been loaded with virtues too refined to be envied and accused of crimes too picturesque to be condemned. Our writers in the past,—the wise men who knew,—informed us that you had bushy tails somewhere hidden in your garments, and often dined off a fricassee of newborn babes! Nay, we had something worse against you: we used to think you the most impracticable people on the earth, for you were said to preach what you never practised.

Such misconceptions are fast vanishing amongst us. Commerce has forced the European tongues on many an Eastern port. Asiatic youths are flocking to Western colleges for the equipment of modern education. Our insight does not penetrate your culture deeply, but at least we are willing to learn. Some of my compatriots have adopted too much of your customs and too much of your etiquette, in the delusion that the acquisition of stiff collars and tall silk hats comprised the attainment of your civilisation. Pathetic and deplorable as such affectations are, they evince our willingness to approach the West on our knees. Unfortunately the Western attitude is unfavourable to the understanding of the East. The Christian missionary goes to impart, but not to receive. Your information is based on the meagre translations of our immense literature, if not on the unreliable anecdotes of passing travellers. It is rarely that the chivalrous pen of a Lafcadio Hearn or that of the author of *The Web of Indian Life*[3] enlivens the Oriental darkness with the torch of our own sentiments.

Perhaps I betray my own ignorance of the Tea Cult by being so outspoken. Its very spirit of politeness exacts that you say what you are expected to say, and no more. But I am not to be a polite Teaist. So much harm has been done already by the mutual misunderstanding of the New World and the Old, that one need not apologise for contributing his tithe to the furtherance of a better understanding. The beginning of the twentieth century would have been spared the spectacle of sanguinary warfare if Russia had condescended to know Japan better. What dire consequences to humanity lie in the contemptuous ignoring of Eastern problems! European imperialism, which does not disdain to raise the absurd cry of the Yellow Peril, fails to realise that Asia may also awaken to the cruel sense of the White Disaster. You may laugh at us for having "too much tea," but may we not suspect that you of the West have "no tea" in your constitution?

Let us stop the continents from hurling epigrams at each other, and be sadder if not wiser by the mutual gain of half a hemisphere. We have developed along different lines, but there is no reason why one should not supplement the other. You have gained expansion at the cost of restlessness; we have created a harmony which is weak against aggression. Will you believe it?—the East is better off in some respects than the West!

Strangely enough, humanity has so far met in the tea-cup. It is the only Asiatic ceremonial which commands universal esteem. The white man has scoffed at our religion and our morals, but has accepted the brown beverage without hesitation. The afternoon tea is now an important function in Western society. In the delicate clatter of trays and saucers, in the soft rustle of feminine hospitality, in the common catechism about cream and sugar, we know that the Worship of Tea is established beyond question. The philosophic resignation of the guest to the fate awaiting him in the dubious decoction proclaims that in this single instance the Oriental spirit reigns supreme.

The earliest record of tea in European writing is said to be found in the statement of an Arabian traveller, that after the year 879 the main sources of

revenue in Canton were the duties on salt and tea.
Marco Polo records the deposition of a Chinese
minister of finance in 1285 for his arbitrary augmenta-
tion of the tea-taxes. It was at the period of the great
discoveries that the European people began to know
more about the extreme Orient. At the end of the
sixteenth century the Hollanders brought the news
that a pleasant drink was made in the East from the
leaves of a bush. The travellers Giovanni Batista
Ramusio (1559), L. Almeida (1576), Maffei (1588),
Taxeira (1610), also mentioned tea. In the last-
named year ships of the Dutch East India Company
brought the first tea into Europe. It was known in
France in 1636, and reached Russia in 1638. England
welcomed it in 1650 and spoke of it as "That
excellent and by all physicians approved China
drink, called by the Chineans Tcha, and by other
nations Tay, alias Tee." [4]

Like all the good things of the world, the propa-
ganda of Tea met with opposition. Heretics like
Henry Sayville (1678) denounced drinking it as a
filthy custom. Jonas Hanway (*Essay on Tea*, 1756) [5]
said that men seemed to lose their stature and come-
liness, women their beauty through the use of tea.
Its cost at the start (about fifteen or sixteen shillings
a pound) forbade popular consumption, and made it
"regalia for high treatments and entertainments,
presents being made thereof to princes and gran-
dees." Yet in spite of such drawbacks tea-drinking
spread with marvellous rapidity. The coffee-houses
of London in the early half of the eighteenth
century became, in fact, tea-houses, the resort of
wits like Addison and Steele, who beguiled themselves over their "dish of tea." The beverage soon
became a necessary of life,—a taxable matter. We
are reminded in this connection what an important

part it plays in modern history. Colonial America resigned herself to oppression until human endurance gave way before the heavy duties laid on Tea. American independence dates from the throwing of tea-chests into Boston harbour.

There is a subtle charm in the taste of tea which makes it irresistible and capable of idealisation. Western humourists were not slow to mingle the fragrance of their thought with its aroma. It has not the arrogance of wine, the self-consciousness of coffee, nor the simpering innocence of cocoa. Already in 1711, says the *Spectator*: "I would therefore in a particular manner recommend these my speculations to all well-regulated families that set apart an hour every morning for tea, bread and butter; and would earnestly advise them for their good to order this paper to be punctually served up and to be looked upon as a part of the tea-equipage." Samuel Johnson draws his own portrait as "a hardened and shameless tea-drinker, who for twenty years diluted his meals with only the infusion of the fascinating plant; who with tea amused the evening, with tea solaced the midnight, and with tea welcomed the morning." [6]

Charles Lamb, a professed devotee, sounded the true note of Teaism when he wrote that the greatest pleasure he knew was to do a good action by stealth, and to have it found out by accident. For Teaism is the art of concealing beauty that you may discover it, of suggesting what you dare not reveal. It is the noble secret of laughing at yourself, calmly yet thoroughly, and is thus humour itself,—the smile of philosophy. All genuine humourists may in this sense be called tea-philosophers,—Thackeray, for instance, and, of course, Shakespeare. The poets of the Decadence (when was not the world in decadence?), in their protests against materialism, have, to a certain extent, also opened the way to Teaism. Perhaps nowadays it is in our demure contemplation of the Imperfect that the West and the East can meet in mutual consolation.

The Taoists relate that at the great beginning of the No-Beginning, Spirit and Matter met in mortal combat. At last the Yellow Emperor, the Son of Heaven, triumphed over Shuhyung [Chu Yung] the demon of darkness and earth. The Titan, in his death agony, struck his head against the solar vault and shivered the blue dome of jade into fragments. The stars lost their nests, the moon wandered aimlessly among the wild chasms of the night. In despair the Yellow Emperor sought far and wide for the repairer of the Heavens. He had not to search in vain. Out of the Eastern sea rose a queen, the divine Niuka [Nü Wa], horn-crowned and dragon-tailed, resplendent in her armour of fire. She welded the five-coloured rainbow in her magic cauldron and rebuilt the Chinese sky. But it is also told that Niuka [Nü Wa] forgot to fill two tiny crevices in the blue firmament. Thus began the dualism of love,—two souls rolling through space and never at rest until they join together to complete the universe. Everyone has to build anew his sky of hope and peace.[7]

The heaven of modern humanity is indeed shattered in the Cyclopean struggle for wealth and power. The world is groping in the shadow of egotism and vulgarity. Knowledge is bought through a bad conscience, benevolence practised for the sake of utility. The East and West, like two dragons tossed in a sea of ferment, in vain strive to regain the jewel of life. We need a Niuka [Nü Wa] again to repair the grand devastation; we await the great

Avatar.[8] Meanwhile, let us have a sip of tea. The afternoon glow is brightening the bamboos, the fountains are bubbling with delight, the soughing of the pines is heard in our kettle. Let us dream of evanescence, and linger in the beautiful foolishness of things.

II. THE SCHOOLS OF TEA

Tea is a work of art and needs a master hand to bring out its noblest qualities. We have good and bad tea, as we have good and bad paintings,—generally the latter. There is no single recipe for making the perfect tea, as there are no rules for producing a Titian or a Sesson.⁹ Each preparation of the leaves has its individuality, its special affinity with water and heat, its hereditary memories to recall, its own method of telling a story. The truly beautiful must be always in it. How much do we not suffer through the constant failure of society to recognise this simple and fundamental law of art and life; Lichihlai [Li Chi Lai],¹⁰ a Sung poet, has sadly remarked that there were three most deplorable things in the world: the spoiling of fine youths through false education, the degradation of fine paintings through vulgar admiration, and the utter waste of fine tea through incompetent manipulation.

Like Art, Tea has its periods and its schools. Its evolution may be roughly divided into three main stages: the Boiled Tea, the Whipped Tea, and the Steeped Tea. We moderns belong to the last school. These several methods of appreciating the beverage are indicative of the spirit of the age in which they prevailed. For life is an expression, our unconscious actions the constant betrayal of our innermost thought. Confucius said that "man hideth not." Perhaps we reveal ourselves too much in small things because we have so little of the great to conceal. The tiny incidents of daily routine are as much a commentary of racial ideals as the highest flight of philosophy or poetry. Even as the difference in favourite vintage marks the separate idiosyncrasies of different periods and nationalities of Europe, so the Tea-ideals characterise the various moods of Oriental culture. The Cake-tea which was boiled, the Powdered-tea which was whipped, the Leaf-tea which was steeped, mark the distinct emotional impulses of the T'ang, the Sung, and the Ming dynasties of China.[11] If we were inclined to borrow the much-abused terminology of art-classification, we might designate them respectively, the Classic, the Romantic, and the Naturalistic schools of Tea.

The tea-plant, a native of southern China, was known from very early times to Chinese botany and medicine. It is alluded to in the classics under the various names of T'o, She, Ch'uan, Chia, and Ming, and was highly prized for possessing the virtues of relieving fatigue, delighting the soul, strengthening the will, and repairing the eyesight. It was not only administered as an internal dose, but often applied externally in the form of paste to alleviate rheumatic pains. The Taoists claimed it as an important ingredient of the elixir of immortality. The Buddhists used it extensively to prevent drowsiness during their long hours of meditation.

By the fourth and fifth centuries Tea became a favourite beverage among the inhabitants of the Yangtse-Kiang valley. It was about this time that the modern ideograph Ch'a was coined, evidently a corruption of the classic T'ou. The poets of the southern dynasties have left some fragments of their fervent adoration of the "froth of the liquid jade." Then emperors used to bestow some rare preparation of the leaves on their high ministers as a reward for eminent services. Yet the method of drinking tea at this stage was primitive in the extreme. The leaves were steamed, crushed in a mortar, made into a cake, and boiled together with rice, ginger, salt, orange peel, spices, milk, and sometimes with onions![12] The custom obtains at the present day among the Thibetans and various Mongolian tribes, who make a curious syrup of these ingredients. The use of lemon slices by the Russians, who learned to take tea from the Chinese caravansaries, points to the survival of the ancient method.

It needed the genius of the T'ang dynasty to emancipate Tea from its crude state and lead to its final idealisation. With Lu Wu [13] in the middle of the eighth century we have our first apostle of tea. He was born in an age when Buddhism, Taoism, and Confucianism were seeking mutual synthesis. The pantheistic symbolism of the time was urging one to mirror the Universal in the Particular. Lu Wu, a poet, saw in the Tea-service the same harmony and order which reigned through all things. In his celebrated work, the *Ch'a Ching* (*The Holy Scripture of Tea*) he formulated the Code of Tea. He has since been worshipped as the tutelary god of the Chinese tea-merchants.

The *Ch'a Ching* consists of three volumes and ten chapters. In the first chapter Lu Wu treats of the nature of the tea-plant, in the second of the implements for gathering the leaves, in the third of the selection of the leaves. According to him the best quality of the leaves must have "creases like the leathern boot of Tartar horsemen, curl like the dewlap of a mighty bullock, unfold like a mist rising out of a ravine, gleam like a lake touched by a zephyr, and be wet and soft like fine earth newly swept by rain."

The fourth chapter is devoted to the enumeration and description of the twenty-four members of the tea-equipage, beginning with the tripod brazier and ending with the bamboo cabinet for containing all these utensils. Here we notice Lu Wu's predilection for Taoist symbolism. Also it is interesting to observe in this connection the influence of tea on Chinese ceramics. The Celestial porcelain, as is well known, had its origin in an attempt to reproduce the exquisite shade of jade, resulting, in the T'ang dynasty, in the blue glaze of the south, and the white glaze of the north. Lu Wu considered the blue as the ideal colour for the tea-cup, as it lent additional greenness to the beverage, whereas the white made it look pinkish and distasteful. It was because he used cake-tea. Later on, when the tea-masters of Sung took to the powdered tea, they preferred heavy bowls of blue-black and dark brown. The Mings, with their steeped tea, rejoiced in light ware of white porcelain.

In the fifth chapter Lu Wu describes the method of making tea. He eliminates all ingredients except salt. He dwells also on the much-discussed question of the choice of water and the degree of boiling it. According to him, the mountain spring is the best, the river water and the spring water come next in the order of excellence. There are three stages of boiling: the first boil is when the little bubbles like the eye of fishes swim on the surface; the second boil is when the bubbles are like crystal beads rolling in a fountain; the third boil is when the billows surge wildly in the kettle. The Cake-tea is roasted before the fire until it becomes soft like a baby's arm and is shredded into powder between pieces of fine paper. Salt is put in the first boil, the tea in the second. At the third boil, a dipperful of cold water is poured into the kettle to settle the tea and revive the "youth of the water." Then the beverage is poured into cups and drunk. O nectar! The filmy leaflets hung like scaly clouds in a serene sky or floated like water-lilies on emerald streams. It was of such a beverage that Lu T'ung, a T'ang poet, wrote: "The first cup moistens my lips and throat, the second cup breaks my loneliness, the third cup searches my barren entrails but to find therein some five thousand volumes of odd ideographs. The fourth cup raises a slight perspiration,—all the wrong of life passes away through my pores. At the fifth cup I am purified; the sixth cup calls me to the realms of immortals. The seventh cup,—ah, but I could take no more! I only feel the breath of cool wind that rises in my sleeves. Where is Horaisan?[14] Let me ride on this sweet breeze and waft away thither."

The remaining chapters of the *Ch'a Ching* treat of the vulgarity of the ordinary methods of tea-drinking, a historical summary of illustrious tea-drinkers, the famous tea plantations of China, the possible variations of the tea-service, and illustrations of the tea-utensils. The last is unfortunately lost.

The appearance of the *Ch'a Ching* must have created considerable sensation at the time. Lu Wu was befriended by the Emperor T'ai Tsung (763–779), and his fame attracted many followers. Some exquisites were said to have been able to detect the tea made by Lu Wu from that of his disciples. One mandarin has his name immortalised by his failure to appreciate the tea of this great master.

In the Sung dynasty the whipped tea came into fashion and created the second school of Tea. The leaves were ground to fine powder in a small stone mill, and the preparation was whipped in hot water by a delicate whisk make of split bamboo. The new process led to some change in the tea-equipage of

Lu Wu, as well as the choice of leaves. Salt was discarded forever. The enthusiasm of the Sung people for tea knew no bounds. Epicures vied with each other in discovering new varieties, and regular tournaments were held to decide their superiority. The Emperor Huei Tsung (1101–1124), who was too great an artist to be a well-behaved monarch, lavished his treasures on the attainment of rare species. He himself wrote a dissertation on the twenty kinds of tea, among which he prizes the "white tea" as of the rarest and finest quality.

The tea-ideal of the Sungs differed from the T'angs' even as their notions of life differed. They sought to actualise what their predecessors tried to symbolise. To the Neo-Confucian mind the cosmic law was not reflected in the phenomenal world, but the phenomenal world was the cosmic law itself. Aeons were but moments,—Nirvana always within grasp. The Taoist conception that immortality lay in the eternal change permeated all their modes of thought. It was the process, not the deed, which was interesting. It was the completing, not the completion, which was really vital. Man came thus at once face to face with nature. A new meaning grew into the art of life. The tea began to be not a poetical pastime, but one of the methods of self-realisation. Wang Yüan Chih eulogised tea as "flooding his soul like a direct appeal, that its delicate bitterness reminded him of the after-taste of a good counsel." Sotumpa [Su Tung-p'o] wrote of the strength of the immaculate purity in tea which defied corruption as a truly virtuous man. Among the Buddhists, the southern Zen sect, which incorporated so much of Taoist doctrines, formulated an elaborate ritual of tea. The monks gathered before the image of

Bodhidharma [15] and drank tea out of a single bowl with the profound formality of a holy sacrament. It was this Zen ritual which finally developed into the Tea-ceremony of Japan in the fifteenth century.

Unfortunately, the sudden outburst of the Mongol tribes in the thirteenth century, which resulted in the devastation and conquest of China under the barbaric rule of the Yuen Emperors, destroyed all the fruits of Sung culture. The native dynasty of the Mings which attempted re-nationalisation in the middle of the fifteenth century was harassed by internal troubles, and China fell under the alien rule of the Manchus in the seventeenth century. Manners and customs changed to leave no vestige of the former times. The powdered tea is entirely forgotten. We find a Ming commentator at loss to recall the shape of the tea whisk mentioned in one of the Sung classics. Tea is now taken by steeping the leaves in hot water in a bowl or cup. The reason why the Western world is innocent of the older method of drinking tea is found in the fact that Europe knew it only at the close of the Ming dynasty.

To the latter-day Chinese tea is a delicious beverage, but not an ideal. The long woes of his country have robbed him of the zest for the meaning of life. He has become modern, that is to say, old and disenchanted. He has lost that sublime faith in illusions which constitutes the eternal youth and vigour of the poets and ancients. He is an eclectic and politely accepts the traditions of the universe. He toys with Nature, but does not condescend to conquer or worship her. His Leaf-tea is often wonderful with its flower-like aroma, but the romance of the T'ang and Sung ceremonials is not to be found in his cup.

Japan, which followed closely on the footsteps of

Chinese civilisation, has known tea in all its three stages. As early as the year 729 we read of the Emperor Shomu giving tea to one hundred monks at his palace in Nara. The leaves were probably imported by our ambassadors to the T'ang Court and prepared in the way then in fashion. In 801 the monk Saicho[16] brought back some seeds and planted them in Yeisan. Many tea-gardens are heard of in the succeeding centuries, as well as the delight of the aristocracy and priesthood in the beverage. The Sung tea reached us in 1191 with the return of Eisai Zenji, who went there to study the southern Zen school. The new seeds which he carried home were successfully planted in three places, one of which, the Uji district near Kyoto, bears still the name of producing the best tea in the world. The southern Zen spread with marvellous rapidity, and with it the tea-ritual and the tea-ideal of the Sung. By the fifteenth century, under the patronage of the Shogun, Ashikaga Yoshimasa, the tea-ceremony is fully constituted and made into an independent and secular performance. Since then Teaism is fully established in Japan. The use of the steeped tea of the later China is comparatively recent among us, being known only since the middle of the seventeenth century. It has replaced the powdered tea in ordinary consumption, though the latter still continues to hold its place as the tea of teas.

It is in the Japanese tea-ceremony that we see the culmination of tea-ideals. Our successful resistance of the Mongol invasion in 1281 had enabled us to carry on the Sung movement, so disastrously cut off in China itself through the nomadic inroad. Tea with us became more than an idealisation of the form of drinking; it is a religion of the art of life. The beverage grew to be an excuse for the worship of purity and refinement, a sacred function at which the host and guest joined to produce for that occasion the utmost beatitude of the mundane. The tea-room was an oasis in the dreary waste of existence where weary travellers could meet to drink from the common spring of art-appreciation. The ceremony was an improvised drama whose plot was woven about the tea, the flowers, and the paintings. Not a colour to disturb the tone of the room, not a sound to mar the rhythm of things, not a gesture to obtrude on the harmony, not a word to break the unity of the surroundings, all movements to be performed simply and naturally,—such were the aims of the tea-ceremony. And strangely enough it was often successful. A subtle philosophy lay behind it all. Teaism was Taoism in disguise.

III. TAOISM AND ZENNISM

The connection of Zennism with tea is proverbial.
We have already remarked that the tea-ceremony was
a development of the Zen ritual. The name of
Lao Tzŭ, the founder of Taoism, is also intimately
associated with the history of tea. It is written in
the Chinese school manual concerning the origin of
habits and customs that the ceremony of offering tea
to a guest began with Kwanyin [Yin Hsi],[17] a well-
known disciple of Lao Tzŭ, who first at the gate of
the Han Pass presented to the "Old Philosopher" a
cup of the golden elixir. We shall not stop to discuss
the authenticity of such tales, which are valuable,
however, as confirming the early use of the beverage
by the Taoists. Our interest in Taoism and Zennism
here lies mainly in those ideas regarding life and art
which are so embodied in what we call Teaism.

It is to be regretted that as yet there appears to be
no adequate presentation of the Taoist and Zen
doctrines in any foreign language, though we have
had several laudable attempts.

Translation is always a treason, and as a Ming
author observes, can at its best be only the reverse
side of a brocade,—all the threads are there, but not
the subtlety of colour or design. But, after all, what
great doctrine is there which is easy to expound?
The ancient sages never put their teachings in
systematic form. They spoke in paradoxes, for they
were afraid of uttering half-truths. They began by

talking like fools and ended by making their hearers wise. Lao Tzŭ himself, with his quaint humour, says, "If people of inferior intelligence hear of the Tao, they laugh immensely. It would not be the Tao unless they laughed at it."

The Tao literally means a Path. It has been severally translated as the Way, the Absolute, the Law, Nature, Supreme Reason, the Mode. These renderings are not incorrect, for the use of the term by the Taoists differs according to the subject-matter of the inquiry. Lao Tzŭ himself spoke of it thus: "There is a thing which is all-containing, which was born before the existence of Heaven and Earth. How silent! How solitary! It stands alone and changes not. It revolves without danger to itself and is the mother of the universe. I do not know its name and so call it the Path. With reluctance I call it the Infinite. Infinity is the Fleeting, the Fleeting is the Vanishing, the Vanishing is the Reverting." The Tao is in the Passage rather than the Path. It is the spirit of Cosmic Change,—the eternal growth which returns upon itself to produce new forms. It recoils upon itself like the dragon, the beloved symbol of the Taoists. It folds and unfolds as do the clouds. The Tao might be spoken of as the Great Transition. Subjectively it is the Mood of the Universe. Its Absolute is the Relative.

It should be remembered in the first place that Taoism, like its legitimate successor Zennism, represents the individualistic trend of the Southern Chinese mind in contra-distinction to the communism of Northern China which expressed itself in Confucianism. The Middle Kingdom is as vast as Europe and has a differentiation of idiosyncrasies marked by the two great river systems which traverse it. The Yangtse-Kiang and Hoang-Ho are respectively the Mediterranean and the Baltic. Even to-day, in spite of centuries of unification, the Southern Celestial differs in his thoughts and beliefs from his Northern brother as a member of the Latin race differs from the Teuton. In ancient days, when communication was even more difficult than at present, and especially during the feudal period, this difference in thought was most pronounced. The art and poetry of the one breathes an atmosphere entirely distinct from that of the other. In Lao Tzŭ and his followers and in Kutsugen [Ch'ü Yüan], the forerunner of the Yangtse-Kiang nature-poets, we find an idealism quite inconsistent with the prosaic ethical notions of their contemporary northern writers. Lao Tzŭ lived five centuries before the Christian Era.

The germ of Taoist speculation may be found long before the advent of Lao Tzŭ, surnamed the Long-Eared. The archaic records of China, especially the *Book of Changes*, foreshadow his thought. But the great respect paid to the laws and customs of that classic period of Chinese civilisation which culminated with the establishment of the Chou dynasty in the sixteenth century B.C., kept the development of individualism in check for a long while, so that it was not until after the disintegration of the Chou dynasty and the establishment of innumerable independent kingdoms that it was able to blossom forth in the luxuriance of free-thought. Lao Tzŭ and Soshi [Chuang Tzŭ] were both Southerners and the greatest exponents of the New School. On the other hand Confucius with his numerous disciples aimed at retaining ancestral conventions. Taoism cannot be understood without some knowledge of Confucianism and vice versa.[18]

We have said that the Taoist Absolute was the

Relative. In ethics the Taoists railed at the laws and the moral codes of society, for to them right and wrong were but relative terms. Definition is always limitation,—the "fixed" and "unchangeless" are but terms expressive of a stoppage of growth. Said Kutsugen [Ch'ü Yüan]: "The Sages move the world." Our standards of morality are begotten of the past needs of society, but is society to remain always the same? The observance of communal traditions involves a constant sacrifice of the individual to the state. Education, in order to keep up the mighty delusion, encourages a species of ignorance. People are not taught to be really virtuous, but to behave properly. We are wicked because we are frightfully self-conscious. We never forgive others because we know that we ourselves are in the wrong. We nurse a conscience because we are afraid to tell the truth to others; we take refuge in pride because we are afraid to tell the truth to ourselves. How can one be serious with the world when the world itself is so ridiculous! The spirit of barter is everywhere. Honour and Chastity! Behold the complacent salesman retailing the Good and True. One can even buy a so-called Religion, which is really but common morality sanctified with flowers and music. Rob the Church of her accessories and what remains behind? Yet the trusts thrive marvellously, for the prices are absurdly cheap,—a prayer for a ticket to heaven, a diploma for an honourable citizenship. Hide yourself under a bushel quickly, for if your real usefulness were known to the world you would soon be knocked down to the highest bidder by the public auctioneer. Why do men and women like to advertise themselves so much? Is it not but an instinct derived from the days of slavery?

The virility of the idea lies not less in its power

of breaking through contemporary thought than in its capacity for dominating subsequent movements. Taoism was an active power during the Ch'in dynasty, that epoch of Chinese unification from which we derive the name China. It would be interesting had we time to note its influence on contemporary thinkers, the mathematicians, writers on law and war, the mystics and alchemists and the later nature-poets of the Yangtse-Kiang. We should not even ignore those speculators on Reality who doubted whether a white horse was real because he was white, or because he was solid, nor the Conversationalists of the Six dynasties who, like the Zen philosophers, revelled in discussions concerning the Pure and the Abstract. Above all we should pay homage to Taoism for what it has done toward the formation of the Celestial character, giving to it a certain capacity for reserve and refinement as "warm as jade." Chinese history is full of instances in which the votaries of Taoism, princes and hermits alike, followed with varied and interesting results the teachings of their creed. The tale will not be without its quota of instruction and amusement. It will be rich in anecdotes, allegories, and aphorisms. We would fain be on speaking terms with the delightful emperor who never died because he never lived. We may ride the wind with Lieh Tzŭ[19] and find it absolutely quiet because we ourselves are the wind, or dwell in mid-air with the Aged One of the Hoang-Ho, who lived betwixt Heaven and Earth because he was subject to neither the one nor the other. Even in that grotesque apology for Taoism which we find in China at the present day, we can revel in a wealth of imagery impossible to find in any other cult.

But the chief contribution of Taoism to Asiatic life has been in the realm of aesthetics. Chinese historians have always spoken of Taoism as the "art of being in the world," for it deals with the present,—ourselves. It is in us that God meets with Nature, and yesterday parts from to-morrow. The Present is the moving Infinity, the legitimate sphere of the Relative. Relativity seeks Adjustment; Adjustment is Art. The art of life lies in a constant readjustment to our surroundings. Taoism accepts the mundane as it is and, unlike the Confucians and the Buddhists, tries to find beauty in our world of woe and worry. The Sung allegory of the Three Vinegar Tasters explains admirably the trend of the three doctrines. Sakyamuni, Confucius, and Lao Tzŭ once stood before a jar of vinegar,—the emblem of life,—and each dipped in his finger to taste the brew. The matter-of-fact Confucius found it sour, the Buddha called it bitter, and Lao Tzŭ pronounced it sweet.

The Taoists claimed that the comedy of life could be made more interesting if everyone would preserve the unities. To keep the proportion of things and give place to others without losing one's own position was the secret of success in the mundane drama. We must know the whole play in order to properly act our parts; the conception of totality must never be lost in that of the individual. This Lao Tzŭ illustrates by his favourite metaphor of the Vacuum. He claimed that only in vacuum lay the truly essential. The reality of a room, for instance, was to be found in the vacant space enclosed by the roof and walls, not in the roof and walls themselves. The usefulness of a water pitcher dwelt in the emptiness where water might be put, not in the form of the pitcher or the material of which it was made. Vacuum is all-potent because all-containing. In vacuum alone motion becomes possible. One who could make of himself a vacuum into which others might freely enter would become master of all situations. The whole can always dominate the part.

These Taoists' ideas have greatly influenced all our theories of action, even to those of fencing and wrestling. Jiu-jitsu, the Japanese art of self-defence, owes its name to a passage in the *Tao-te-king*. In jiu-jitsu one seeks to draw out and exhaust the enemy's strength by non-resistance, vacuum, while conserving one's own strength for victory in the final struggle. In art the importance of the same principle is illustrated by the value of suggestion. In leaving something unsaid the beholder is given a chance to complete the idea and thus a great master-piece irresistibly rivets your attention until you seem to become actually a part of it. A vacuum is there for you to enter and fill up to the full measure of your aesthetic emotion.

He who had made himself master of the art of living was the Real Man of the Taoist. At birth he enters the realm of dreams only to awaken to reality at death. He tempers his own brightness in order to merge himself into the obscurity of others. He is "reluctant, as one who crosses a stream in winter; hesitating, as one who fears the neighbourhood; respectful, like a guest; trembling, like ice that is about to melt; unassuming, like a piece of wood not yet carved; vacant, like a valley; formless, like troubled waters." To him the three jewels of life were Pity, Economy, and Modesty.

If now we turn our attention to Zennism we shall find that it emphasises the teachings of Taoism. Zen is a name derived from the Sanscrit word Dhyana, which signifies meditation. It claims that through consecrated meditation may be attained supreme self-realisation. Meditation is one of the six ways through which Buddhahood may be reached, and the Zen sectarians affirm that Sakyamuni laid special stress on this method in his later teachings, handing down the rules to his chief disciple Kasyapa. According to their tradition Kasyapa, the first Zen patriarch, imparted the secret to Ananda, who in turn passed it on to successive patriarchs until it reached Bodhidharma, the twenty-eighth. Bodhidharma came to Northern China in the early half of the sixth century and was the first patriarch of Chinese Zen. There is much uncertainty about the history of these patriarchs and their doctrines. In its philosophical aspect early Zennism seems to have affinity on one hand to the Indian Negativism of Nagarjuna and on the other to Jñana philosophy formulated by Sankaracharya. The first teaching of Zen as we know it at the present day must be attributed to the sixth Chinese patriarch Enō [Hui-nêng] (637–713), founder of Southern Zen, so-called from the fact of its predominance in Southern China. He is closely followed by the great Baso [Ma-tsu] (died 788) who made of Zen a living influence in Celestial life. Hyakujō [Pai-chang] (719–814) the pupil of Baso, first instituted the Zen monastery and established a ritual and regulations for its government. In the discussions of the Zen school after the time of Baso we find the play of the Yangtse-Kiang mind causing an accession of native modes of thought in contrast to the former Indian idealism. Whatever sectarian pride may assert to the contrary, one cannot help being impressed by the similarity of Southern Zen to the teachings of Lao Tzŭ and the Taoist Conversationalists. In the *Tao-te-king* we already find allusions to the importance of self-concentration and the need of properly regulating the breath,—essential points in the

practice of Zen meditation. Some of the best
commentaries on the *Book of Lao Tzŭ* have been
written by Zen scholars.

Zennism, like Taoism, is the worship of Relativity.
One master defines Zen as the art of feeling the polar
star in the southern sky. Truth can be reached only
through the comprehension of opposites. Again,
Zennism, like Taoism, is a strong advocate of
individualism. Nothing is real except that which con-
cerns the working of our own minds. Enō [Hui-nêng],
the sixth patriarch, once saw two monks watching
the flag of a pagoda fluttering in the wind. One said
"It is the wind that moves," the other said "It is the
flag that moves"; but Enō explained to them that the
real movement was neither of the wind nor the flag,
but of something within their own minds. Hyakujō
[Pai-chang] was walking in the forest with a disciple
when a hare scurried off at their approach. "Why
does the hare fly from you?" asked Hyakujō.
"Because he is afraid of me," was the answer.
"No," said the master, "it is because you have a
murderous instinct." This dialogue recalls that of
Soshi [Chuang Tzŭ], the Taoist. One day Soshi was
walking on the bank of a river with a friend. "How
delightfully the fishes are enjoying themselves in the
water!" exclaimed Soshi. His friend spake to him
thus: "You are not a fish; how do you know that the
fishes are enjoying themselves?" "You are not
myself," returned Soshi; "how do you know that I
do not know that the fishes are enjoying themselves?"

Zen was often opposed to the precepts of orthodox
Buddhism even as Taoism was opposed to Confucianism. To the transcendental insight of the Zen,
words were but an incumbrance to thought, the
whole sway of Buddhist scriptures only commentaries on personal speculation. The followers of Zen

aimed at direct communion with the inner nature of things, regarding their outward accessories only as impediments to a clear perception of Truth. It was this love of the Abstract that led the Zen to prefer black and white sketches to the elaborately coloured paintings of the classic Buddhist School. Some of the Zen even became iconoclastic as a result of their endeavour to recognise the Buddha in themselves rather than through images and symbolism. We find Tanka Osho [Tan Hsia] breaking up a wooden statue of Buddha on a wintry day to make a fire. "What sacrilege!" said the horror-stricken by-stander. "I wish to get the Shali out of the ashes," calmly rejoined the Zen. "But you certainly will not get Shali from this image!" was the angry retort, to which Tanka replied, "If I do not, this is certainly not a Buddha and I am committing no sacrilege." Then he turned to warm himself over the kindling fire.[20]

A special contribution of Zen to Eastern thought was its recognition of the mundane as of equal importance with the spiritual. It held that in the great relation of things there was no distinction of small and great, an atom possessing equal possibilities with the universe. The seeker for perfection must discover in his own life the reflection of the inner light. The organisation of the Zen monastery was very significant of this point of view. To every member, except the abbot, was assigned some special work in the caretaking of the monastery, and curiously enough, to the novices were committed the lighter duties, while to the most respected and advanced monks were given the more irksome and menial tasks. Such services formed a part of the Zen discipline and every least action had to be done absolutely perfectly. Thus many a weighty discussion ensued while weeding the garden, paring a turnip, or serving tea. The whole ideal of Teaism is a result of this Zen conception of greatness in the smallest incidents of life. Taoism furnished the basis for aesthetic ideals, Zennism made them practical.

IV. THE TEA-ROOM

To European architects brought up on the traditions of stone and brick construction, our Japanese method of building with wood and bamboo seems scarcely worthy to be ranked as architecture. It is but quite recently that a competent student of Western architecture has recognised and paid tribute to the remarkable perfection of our great temples.* Such being the case as regards our classic architecture, we could hardly expect the outsider to appreciate the subtle beauty of the tea-room, its principles of construction and decoration being entirely different from those of the West.

The tea-room (the Sukiya) does not pretend to be other than a mere cottage,—a straw hut, as we call it. The original ideographs for Sukiya mean the Abode of Fancy. Latterly the various tea-masters substituted various Chinese characters according to their conception of the tea-room, and the term Sukiya may signify the Abode of Vacancy or the Abode of the Unsymmetrical. It is an Abode of Fancy inasmuch as it is an ephemeral structure built to house a poetic impulse. It is an Abode of Vacancy inasmuch as it is devoid of ornamentation except for what may be placed in it to satisfy some aesthetic need of the moment. It is an Abode of the Unsymmetrical inasmuch as it is consecrated to the

* We refer to Ralph N. Cram's *Impressions of Japanese Architecture and the Allied Arts.* The Baker & Taylor Co., New York, 1905.

worship of the Imperfect, purposely leaving some
thing unfinished for the play of the imagination to
complete.[21] The ideals of Teaism have since the
sixteenth century influenced our architecture to
such a degree that the ordinary Japanese interior of
the present day, on account of the extreme simplicity
and chasteness of its scheme of decoration, appears
to foreigners almost barren.

The first independent tea-room was the creation
of Sen-no-Sōeki, commonly known by his later
name of Rikyu, the greatest of all tea-masters, who,
in the sixteenth century, under the patronage of
Taikō Hideyoshi,[22] instituted and brought to a
high state of perfection the formalities of the Tea-
ceremony. The proportions of the tea-room had
been previously determined by Shō-Ō,—a famous
tea-master of the fifteenth century. The early tea-
room consisted merely of a portion of the ordinary
drawing-room partitioned off by screens for the
purpose of the tea-gathering. The portion partitioned off was called the Kakoi (enclosure), a name
still applied to those tea-rooms which are built into a
house and are not independent constructions. The
Sukiya consists of the tea-room proper, designed to
accommodate not more than five persons, a number
suggestive of the saying "more than the Graces and
less than the Muses," an anteroom (mizuya) where
the tea-utensils are washed and arranged before
being brought in, a portico (machiai) in which the
guests wait until they receive the summons to enter
the tea-room, and a garden path (the rōji) which
connects the machiai with the tea-room. The tea-
room is unimpressive in appearance. It is smaller
than the smallest of Japanese houses, while the
materials used in its construction are intended to
give the suggestion of refined poverty. Yet we must

remember that all this is the result of profound artistic forethought, and that the details have been worked out with care perhaps even greater than that expended on the building of the richest palaces and temples. A good tea-room is more costly than an ordinary mansion, for the selection of its materials, as well as its workmanship, requires immense care and precision. Indeed, the carpenters employed by the tea-masters form a distinct and highly honoured class among artisans, their work being no less delicate than that of the makers of lacquer cabinets.

The tea-room is not only different from any production of Western architecture, but also contrasts strongly with the classical architecture of Japan itself. Our ancient noble edifices, whether secular or ecclesiastical, were not to be despised even as regards their mere size. The few that have been spared in the disastrous conflagrations of centuries are still capable of awing us by the grandeur and richness of their decoration. Huge pillars of wood, from two to three feet in diameter and from thirty to forty feet high, supported, by a complicated network of brackets, the enormous beams which groaned under the weight of the tile-covered slanting roofs. The material and mode of construction, though weak against fire, proved itself strong against earthquakes, and was well suited to the climatic conditions of the country. In the Golden Hall of Horyuji and the Pagoda of Yakushiji, we have noteworthy examples of the durability of our wooden architecture. These buildings have practically stood intact for nearly twelve centuries. The interior of the old temples and palaces was profusely decorated. In the Hōōdo temple at Uji, dating from the tenth century, we can still see the elaborate canopy and gilded baldachinos, many-coloured and inlaid with mirrors and mother-of-pearl, as well as remains of the paintings and sculpture which formerly covered the walls. Later, at Nikko and in the Nijo castle in Kyoto, we see structural beauty sacrificed to a wealth of ornamentation which in colour and exquisite detail equals the utmost gorgeousness of Arabian or Moorish effort.

The simplicity and purism of the tea-room resulted from emulation of the Zen monastery. A Zen monastery differs from those of other Buddhist sects inasmuch as it is meant only to be a dwelling place for the monks. Its chapel is not a place of worship or pilgrimage, but a college room where the students congregate for discussion and the practice of meditation. The room is bare except for a central alcove in which, behind the altar, is a statue of Bodhidharma, the founder of the sect, or of Sakyamuni attended by Kasyapa and Ananda,[23] the two earliest Zen patriarchs. On the altar, flowers and incense are offered up in memory of the great contributions which these sages made to Zen. We have already said that it was the ritual instituted by the Zen monks of successively drinking tea out of a bowl before the image of Bodhidharma, which laid the foundations of the tea-ceremony. We might add here that the altar of the Zen chapel was the prototype of the Tokonoma,—the place of honour in a Japanese room where paintings and flowers are placed for the edification of the guests.

All our great tea-masters were students of Zen and attempted to introduce the spirit of Zennism into the actualities of life. Thus the room, like the other equipments of the tea-ceremony, reflects many of the Zen doctrines. The size of the orthodox tea-room, which is four mats and a half, or ten feet square, is determined by a passage in the Sutra of Vikramaditya. In that interesting work, Vikramaditya welcomes the Saint Manjusri [24] and eighty-four thousand disciples of Buddha in a room of this size,—an allegory based on the theory of the non-existence of space to the truly enlightened. Again the rōji, the garden path which leads from the machiai to the tea-room, signified the first stage of meditation, —the passage into self-illumination. The rōji was intended to break connection with the outside world, and to produce a fresh sensation conducive to the full enjoyment of aestheticism in the tea-room itself. One who has trodden this garden path cannot fail to remember how his spirit, as he walked in the twilight of evergreens over the regular irregularities of the stepping stones, beneath which lay dried pine needles, and passed beside the moss-covered granite lanterns, became uplifted above ordinary thoughts. One may be in the midst of a city, and yet feel as if he were in the forest far away from the dust and din of civilisation. Great was the ingenuity displayed by the tea-masters in producing these effects of serenity and purity. The nature of the sensations to be aroused in passing through the rōji differed with different tea-masters. Some, like Rikyu, aimed at utter loneliness, and claimed the secret of making a rōji was contained in the ancient ditty:

> I look beyond;
> Flowers are not,
> Nor tinted leaves.
> On the sea beach
> A solitary cottage stands
> In the waning light
> Of an autumn eve.

Others, like Kobori Enshu, sought for a different effect. Enshu said the idea of the garden path was to be found in the following verses:

> A cluster of summer trees,
> A bit of the sea,
> A pale evening moon.

It is not difficult to gather his meaning. He wished to create the attitude of a newly awakened soul still lingering amid shadowy dreams of the past, yet bathing in the sweet unconsciousness of a mellow spiritual light, and yearning for the freedom that lay in the expanse beyond.

Thus prepared the guest will silently approach the sanctuary, and, if a samurai, will leave his sword on the rack beneath the eaves, the tea-room being preëminently the house of peace. Then he will bend low and creep into the room through a small door not more than three feet in height. This proceeding was incumbent on all guests,—high and low alike,—and was intended to inculcate humility. The order of precedence having been mutually agreed upon while resting in the machiai, the guests one by one will enter noiselessly and take their seats, first making obeisance to the picture or flower arrangement on the tokonoma. The host will not enter the room until all the guests have seated themselves and quiet reigns with nothing to break the silence save the note of the boiling water in the iron kettle. The kettle sings well, for pieces of iron are so arranged in the bottom as to produce a peculiar melody in which one may hear the echoes of a cataract muffled by clouds, of a distant sea breaking among the rocks, a rainstorm sweeping through a bamboo forest, or of the soughing of pines on some faraway hill.

Even in the daytime the light in the room is subdued, for the low eaves of the slanting roof admit but few of the sun's rays. Everything is sober in tint from the ceiling to the floor; the guests themselves have carefully chosen garments of unobtrusive colours. The mellowness of age is over all, everything suggestive of recent acquirement being tabooed save only the one note of contrast furnished by the bamboo dipper and the linen napkin, both immaculately white and new. However faded the tea-room and the tea-equipage may seem, everything is absolutely clean. Not a particle of dust will be found in the darkest corner, for if any exists the host is not a tea-master. One of the first requisites of a tea-master is the knowledge of how to sweep, clean, and wash, for there is an art in cleaning and dusting. A piece of antique metalwork must not be attacked with the unscrupulous zeal of the Dutch housewife. Dripping water from a flower vase need not be wiped away, for it may be suggestive of dew and coolness.

In this connection there is a story of Rikyu which well illustrates the ideas of cleanliness entertained by the tea-masters. Rikyu was watching his son Sho-an as he swept and watered the garden path. "Not clean enough," said Rikyu, when Sho-an had finished his task, and bade him try again. After a weary hour the son turned to Rikyu: "Father, there is nothing more to be done. The steps have been washed for the third time, the stone lanterns and the trees are well sprinkled with water, moss and lichens are shining with a fresh verdure; not a twig, not a leaf have I left on the ground." "Young fool," chided the tea-master, "that is not the way a garden path should be swept." Saying this, Rikyu stepped into the garden, shook a tree and scattered over the garden gold and crimson leaves, scraps of the brocade of autumn!

What Rikyu demanded was not cleanliness alone, but the beautiful and the natural also.

The name, Abode of Fancy, implies a structure created to meet some individual artistic requirement. The tea-room is made for the tea-master, not the tea-master for the tea-room. It is not intended for posterity and is therefore ephemeral. The idea that everyone should have a house of his own is based on an ancient custom of the Japanese race, Shinto super-stition ordaining that every dwelling should be evacuated on the death of its chief occupant. Perhaps there may have been some unrealised sanitary reason for this practice. Another early custom was that a newly built house should be provided for each couple that married. It is on account of such customs that we find the Imperial capitals so frequently removed from one site to another in ancient days. The rebuilding, every twenty years, of Ise Temple, the supreme shrine of the Sun-Goddess, is an example of one of these ancient rites which still obtain at the present day. The observance of these customs was only possible with some such form of construction as that furnished by our system of wooden architec-ture, easily pulled down, easily built up. A more lasting style, employing brick and stone, would have rendered migrations impracticable, as indeed they became when the more stable and massive wooden construction of China was adopted by us after the Nara period.

With the predominance of Zen individualism in the fifteenth century, however, the old idea became imbued with a deeper significance as conceived in connection with the tea-room. Zennism, with the Buddhist theory of evanescence and its demands for the mastery of spirit over matter, recognised the house only as a temporary refuge for the body. The body itself was but as a hut in the wilderness, a flimsy shelter made by tying together the grasses that grew around,—when these ceased to be bound together they again became resolved into the original waste. In the tea-room fugitiveness is suggested in the thatched roof, frailty in the slender pillars, lightness in the bamboo support, apparent carelessness in the use of commonplace materials. The eternal is to be found only in the spirit which, embodied in these simple surroundings, beautifies them with the subtle light of its refinement.

That the tea-room should be built to suit some individual taste is an enforcement of the principle of vitality in art. Art, to be fully appreciated, must be true to contemporaneous life. It is not that we should ignore the claims of posterity, but that we should seek to enjoy the present more. It is not that we should disregard the creations of the past, but that we should try to assimilate them into our consciousness. Slavish conformity to traditions and formulas fetters the expression of individuality in architecture. We can but weep over those senseless imitations of European buildings which one beholds in modern Japan. We marvel why, among the most progressive Western nations, architecture should be so devoid of originality, so replete with repetitions of obsolete styles. Perhaps we are now passing through an age of democratisation in art, while awaiting the rise of some princely master who shall establish a new dynasty. Would that we loved the ancients more and copied them less! It has been said that the Greeks were great because they never drew from the antique.

The term, Abode of Vacancy, besides conveying the Taoist theory of the all-containing, involves the conception of a continued need of change in decorative motives. The tea-room is absolutely empty, except for what may be placed there temporarily to satisfy some aesthetic mood. Some special art object is brought in for the occasion, and everything else is selected and arranged to enhance the beauty of the principal theme. One cannot listen to different pieces of music at the same time, a real comprehension of the beautiful being possible only through concentration upon some central motive. Thus it will be seen that the system of decoration in our tearooms is opposed to that which obtains in the West, where the interior of a house is often converted into a museum. To a Japanese, accustomed to simplicity of ornamentation and frequent change of decorative method, a Western interior permanently filled with a vast array of pictures, statuary, and bric-à-brac gives the impression of mere vulgar display of riches. It calls for a mighty wealth of appreciation to enjoy the constant sight of even a masterpiece, and limitless indeed must be the capacity for artistic feeling in those who can exist day after day in the midst of such confusion of colour and form as is to be often seen in the homes of Europe and America.

The "Abode of the Unsymmetrical" suggests another phase of our decorative scheme. The absence of symmetry in Japanese art objects has been often commented on by Western critics. This, also, is a result of a working out through Zennism of Taoist ideals. Confucianism, with its deep-seated idea of dualism, and Northern Buddhism with its worship of a trinity, were in no way opposed to the expression of symmetry. As a matter of fact, if we study the ancient bronzes of China or the religious arts of the T'ang dynasty and the Nara period, we shall recognise a constant striving after symmetry. The decoration of our classical interiors was decidedly

regular in its arrangement. The Taoist and Zen
conception of perfection, however, was different.
The dynamic nature of their philosophy laid more
stress upon the process through which perfection
was sought than upon perfection itself. True beauty
could be discovered only by one who mentally
completed the incomplete. The virility of life and art
lay in its possibilities for growth. In the tea-room it
is left for each guest in imagination to complete the
total effect in relation to himself. Since Zennism has
become the prevailing mode of thought, the art of
the extreme Orient has purposely avoided the
symmetrical as expressing not only completion, but
repetition. Uniformity of design was considered as
fatal to the freshness of imagination. Thus, landscapes, birds, and flowers became the favourite
subjects for depiction rather than the human figure,
the latter being present in the person of the beholder
himself. We are often too much in evidence as it is,
and in spite of our vanity even self-regard is apt to
become monotonous.

In the tea-room the fear of repetition is a constant
presence. The various objects for the decoration of a
room should be so selected that no colour or design
shall be repeated. If you have a living flower, a
painting of flowers is not allowable. If you are
using a round kettle, the water pitcher should be
angular. A cup with a black glaze should not be
associated with a tea-caddy of black lacquer. In
placing a vase on an incense burner on the tokonoma,
care should be taken not to put it in the exact centre,
lest it divide the space into equal halves. The pillar of
the tokonoma should be of a different kind of wood
from the other pillars, in order to break any suggestion
of monotony in the room.

Here again the Japanese method of interior

decoration differs from that of the Occident, where we see objects arrayed symmetrically on mantelpieces and elsewhere. In Western houses we are often confronted with what appears to us useless reiteration. We find it trying to talk to a man while his full-length portrait stares at us from behind his back. We wonder which is real, he of the picture or he who talks, and feel a curious conviction that one of them must be fraud. Many a time have we sat at a festive board contemplating, with a secret shock to our digestion, the representation of abundance on the dining-room walls. Why these pictured victims of chase and sport, the elaborate carvings of fishes and fruit? Why the display of family plates, reminding us of those who have dined and are dead?

The simplicity of the tea-room and its freedom from vulgarity make it truly a sanctuary from the vexation of the outer world. There and there alone can one consecrate himself to undisturbed adoration of the beautiful. In the sixteenth century the tea-room afforded a welcome respite from labour to the fierce warriors and statesmen engaged in the unification and reconstruction of Japan. In the seventeenth century, after the strict formalism of the Tokugawa rule had been developed, it offered the only opportunity possible for the free communion of artistic spirits. Before a great work of art there was no distinction between daimyo, samurai, and commoner. Nowadays industrialism is making true refinement more and more difficult all the world over. Do we not need the tea-room more than ever?

V. ART APPRECIATION

Have you heard the Taoist tale of the Taming of the Harp?

Once in the hoary ages in the Ravine of Lung Men * stood a Kiri [Paulownia] tree, a veritable king of the forest. It reared its head to talk to the stars; its roots struck deep into the earth, mingling their bronzed coils with those of the silver dragon that slept beneath. And it came to pass that a mighty wizard made of this tree a wondrous harp, whose stubborn spirit should be tamed but by the greatest of musicians. For long the instrument was treasured by the Emperor of China, but all in vain were the efforts of those who in turn tried to draw melody from its strings. In response to their utmost strivings there came from the harp but harsh notes of disdain, ill-according with the songs they fain would sing. The harp refused to recognise a master.

At last came Pai Ya, the prince of harpists. With tender hand he caressed the harp as one might seek to soothe an unruly horse, and softly touched the chords. He sang of nature and the seasons, of high mountains and flowing waters, and all the memories of the tree awoke! Once more the sweet breath of spring played amidst its branches. The young cataracts, as they danced down the ravine, laughed to the budding flowers. Anon were heard the dreamy voices of summer with its myriad insects, the gentle

*The Dragon Gorge of Honan.

42

pattering of rain, the wail of the cuckoo. Hark! a
tiger roars,—the valley answers again. It is autumn;
in the desert night, sharp like a sword gleams the
moon upon the frosted grass. Now winter reigns, and
through the snow-filled air swirl flocks of swans and
rattling hailstones beat upon the boughs with fierce
delight.

Then Pai Ya changed the key and sang of love.
The forest swayed like an ardent swain deep lost in
thought. On high, like a haughty maiden, swept a
cloud bright and fair; but passing, trailed long
shadows on the ground, black like despair. Again
the mode was changed; Pai Ya sang of war, of
clashing steel and trampling steeds. And in the harp
arose the tempest of Lung Men, the dragon rode
the lightning, the thundering avalanche crashed
through the hills. In ecstasy the Celestial monarch
asked Pai Ya wherein lay the secret of his victory.
"Sire," he replied, "others have failed because they
sang but of themselves. I left the harp to choose its
theme, and knew not truly whether the harp had been
Pai Ya or Pai Ya were the harp."

This story well illustrates the mystery of art
appreciation. The masterpiece is a symphony played
upon our finest feelings. True art is Pai Ya, and we
the harp of Lung Men. At the magic touch of the
beautiful the secret chords of our being are awakened,
we vibrate and thrill in response to its call. Mind
speaks to mind. We listen to the unspoken, we gaze
upon the unseen. The master calls forth notes we
know not of. Memories long forgotten all come back
to us with a new significance. Hopes stifled by fear,
yearnings that we dare not recognise, stand forth in
new glory. Our mind is the canvas on which the
artists lay their colour; their pigments are our
emotions; their chiaroscuro the light of joy, the

shadow of sadness. The masterpiece is of ourselves, as we are of the masterpiece.

The sympathetic communion of minds necessary for art appreciation must be based on mutual concession. The spectator must cultivate the proper attitude for receiving the message, as the artist must know how to impart it. The tea-master, Kobori Enshu, himself a daimyo, has left to us these memorable words: "Approach a great painting as thou wouldst approach a great prince." In order to understand a masterpiece, you must lay yourself low before it and await with bated breath its least utterance. An eminent Sung critic once made a charming confession. Said he: "In my young days I praised the master whose pictures I liked, but as my judgment matured I praised myself for liking what the masters had chosen to have me like." It is to be deplored that so few of us really take pains to study the moods of the masters. In our stubborn ignorance we refuse to render them this simple courtesy, and thus often miss the rich repast of beauty spread before our very eyes. A master has always something to offer, while we go hungry solely because of our own lack of appreciation.

To the sympathetic a masterpiece becomes a living reality towards which we feel drawn in bonds of comradeship. The masters are immortal, for their loves and fears live in us over and over again. It is rather the soul than the hand, the man than the technique, which appeals to us,—the more human the call the deeper is our response. It is because of this secret understanding between the master and ourselves that in poetry or romance we suffer and rejoice with the hero and heroine. Chikamatsu, our Japanese Shakespeare, has laid down as one of the first principles of dramatic composition the importance of taking the audience into the confidence of the author.

Several of his pupils submitted plays for his approval, but only one of the pieces appealed to him. It was a play somewhat resembling the *Comedy of Errors,* in which twin brethren suffer through mistaken identity. "This," said Chikamatsu, "has the proper spirit of the drama, for it takes the audience into consideration. The public is permitted to know more than the actors. It knows where the mistake lies, and pities the poor figures on the board who innocently rush to their fate."

The great masters both of the East and the West never forgot the value of suggestion as a means for taking the spectator into their confidence. Who can contemplate a masterpiece without being awed by the immense vista of thought presented to our consideration? How familiar and sympathetic are they all; how cold in contrast the modern common-places! In the former we feel the warm outpouring of a man's heart, in the latter only a formal salute. Engrossed in his technique, the modern rarely rises above himself. Like the musicians who vainly invoked the Lung Men harp, he sings only of himself. His works may be nearer science, but are further from humanity. We have an old saying in Japan that a woman cannot love a man who is truly vain, for there is no crevice in his heart for love to enter and fill up. In art vanity is equally fatal to sympathetic feeling, whether on the part of the artist or the public.

Nothing is more hallowing than the union of kindred spirits in art. At the moment of meeting, the art lover transcends himself. At once he is and is not. He catches a glimpse of Infinity, but words cannot voice his delight, for the eye has no tongue. Freed from the fetters of matter, his spirit moves in the rhythm of things. It is thus that art becomes akin to religion and ennobles mankind. It is this which makes a masterpiece something sacred. In the old days the veneration in which the Japanese held the work of the great artist was intense. The tea-masters guarded their treasures with religious secrecy, and it was often necessary to open a whole series of boxes, one within another, before reaching the shrine itself,—the silken wrapping within whose soft folds lay the holy of holies. Rarely was the object exposed to view, and then only to the initiated.

At the time when Teaism was in the ascendency the Taiko's generals would be better satisfied with the present of a rare work of art than a large grant of territory as a reward of victory. Many of our favourite dramas are based on the loss and recovery of a noted masterpiece. For instance, in one play the palace of Lord Hosokawa, in which was preserved the celebrated painting of Daruma [Bodhidharma] by Sesson, suddenly takes fire through the negligence of the samurai in charge. Resolved at all hazards to rescue the precious painting, he rushes into the burning building and seizes the kakemono, only to find all means of exit cut off by the flames. Thinking only of the picture, he slashes open his body with his sword, wraps his torn sleeve about the Sesson and plunges it into the gaping wound. The fire is at last extinguished. Among the smoking embers is found a half-consumed corpse, within which reposes the treasure uninjured by the fire. Horrible as such tales are, they illustrate the great value that we set upon a masterpiece, as well as the devotion of a trusted samurai.

We must remember, however, that art is of value only to the extent that it speaks to us. It might be a universal language if we ourselves were universal in our sympathies. Our finite nature, the power of tradition and conventionality, as well as our hereditary instincts, restrict the scope of our capacity for artistic enjoyment. Our very individuality establishes in one sense a limit to our understanding; and our aesthetic personality seeks its own affinities in the creations of the past. It is true that with cultivation our sense of art appreciation broadens, and we become able to enjoy many hitherto unrecognised expressions of beauty. But, after all, we see only our own image in the universe,—our particular idiosyncrasies dictate the mode of our perceptions. The tea-masters collected only objects which fell strictly within the measure of their individual appreciation.

One is reminded in this connection of a story concerning Kobori Enshu. Enshu was complimented by his disciples on the admirable taste he had displayed in the choice of his collection. Said they, "Each piece is such that no one could help admiring. It shows that you had better taste than had Rikyu, for his collection could only be appreciated by one beholder in a thousand." Sorrowfully Enshu replied: "This only proves how commonplace I am. The great Rikyu dared to love only those objects which personally appealed to him, whereas I unconsciously cater to the taste of the majority. Verily, Rikyu was one in a thousand among tea-masters."

It is much to be regretted that so much of the apparent enthusiasm for art at the present day has no foundation in real feeling. In this democratic age of ours men clamour for what is popularly considered the best, regardless of their feelings. They want the costly, not the refined; the fashionable, not the beautiful. To the masses, contemplation of illustrated periodicals, the worthy product of their own industrialism, would give more digestible food for artistic enjoyment than the early Italians or the

Ashikaga masters, whom they pretend to admire. The name of the artist is more important to them than the quality of the work. As a Chinese critic complained many centuries ago, "People criticise a picture by their ear." It is this lack of genuine appreciation that is responsible for the pseudo-classic horrors that to-day greet us wherever we turn.

Another common mistake is that of confusing art with archaeology. The veneration born of antiquity is one of the best traits in the human character, and fain would we have it cultivated to a greater extent. The old masters are rightly to be honoured for opening the path to future enlightenment. The mere fact that they have passed unscathed through centuries of criticism and come down to us still covered with glory commands our respect. But we should be foolish indeed if we valued their achievement simply on the score of age. Yet we allow our historical sympathy to override our aesthetic discrimination. We offer flowers of approbation when the artist is safely laid in his grave. The nineteenth century, pregnant with the theory of evolution, has moreover created in us the habit of losing sight of the individual in the species. A collector is anxious to acquire specimens to illustrate a period or a school, and forgets that a single masterpiece can teach us more than any number of the mediocre products of a given period or school. We classify too much and enjoy too little. The sacrifice of the aesthetic to the so-called scientific method of exhibition has been the bane of many museums.

The claims of contemporary art cannot be ignored in any vital scheme of life. The art of to-day is that which really belongs to us: it is our own reflection. In condemning it we but condemn ourselves. We say that the present age possesses no art:—who is responsible for this ? It is indeed a shame that despite all our rhapsodies about the ancients we pay so little attention to our own possibilities. Struggling artists, weary souls lingering in the shadow of cold disdain! In our self-centred century, what inspiration do we offer them ? The past may well look with pity at the poverty of our civilisation; the future will laugh at the barrenness of our art. We are destroying art in destroying the beautiful in life. Would that some great wizard might from the stem of society shape a mighty harp whose strings would resound to the touch of genius.

VI. FLOWERS

In the trembling grey of a spring dawn, when the birds were whispering in mysterious cadence among the trees, have you not felt that they were talking to their mates about the flowers? Surely with mankind the appreciation of flowers must have been coeval with the poetry of love. Where better than in a flower, sweet in its unconsciousness, fragrant because of its silence, can we image the unfolding of a virgin soul? The primeval man in offering the first garland to his maiden thereby transcended the brute. He became human in thus rising above the crude necessities of nature. He entered the realm of art when he perceived the subtle use of the useless.

In joy or sadness, flowers are our constant friends. We eat, drink, sing, dance, and flirt with them. We wed and christen with flowers. We dare not die without them. We have worshipped with the lily, we have meditated with the lotus, we have charged in battle array with the rose and the chrysanthemum. We have even attempted to speak in the language of flowers. How could we live without them? It frightens one to conceive of a world bereft of their presence. What solace do they not bring to the bed-side of the sick, what a light of bliss to the darkness of weary spirits? Their serene tenderness restores to us our waning confidence in the universe even as the intent gaze of a beautiful child recalls our lost hopes. When we are laid low in the dust it is they who linger in sorrow over our graves.

Sad as it is, we cannot conceal the fact that in spite of our companionship with flowers we have not risen very far above the brute. Scratch the sheepskin and the wolf within us will soon show his teeth. It has been said that man at ten is an animal, at twenty a lunatic, at thirty a failure, at forty a fraud, and at fifty a criminal. Perhaps he becomes a criminal because he has never ceased to be an animal. Nothing is real to us but hunger, nothing sacred except our own desires. Shrine after shrine has crumbled before our eyes; but one altar forever is preserved, that whereon we burn incense to the supreme idol,—ourselves. Our god is great, and money is his Prophet! We devastate nature in order to make sacrifice to him. We boast that we have conquered Matter and forget that it is Matter that has enslaved us. What atrocities do we not perpetrate in the name of culture and refinement!

Tell me, gentle flowers, teardrops of the stars, standing in the garden, nodding your heads to the bees as they sing of the dews and the sunbeams, are you aware of the fearful doom that awaits you? Dream on, sway and frolic while you may in the gentle breezes of summer. To-morrow a ruthless hand will close around your throats. You will be wrenched, torn asunder limb by limb, and borne away from your quiet homes. The wretch, she may be passing fair. She may say how lovely you are while her fingers are still moist with your blood. Tell me, will this be kindness? It may be your fate to be imprisoned in the hair of one whom you know to be heartless or to be thrust into the buttonhole of one who would not dare to look you in the face were you a man. It may even be your lot to be confined in some narrow vessel with only stagnant water to quench the maddening thirst that warns of ebbing life.

Flowers, if you were in the land of the Mikado, you might some time meet a dread personage armed with scissors and a tiny saw. He would call himself a Master of Flowers. He would claim the rights of a doctor and you would instinctively hate him, for you know a doctor always seeks to prolong the troubles of his victims. He would cut, bend, and twist you into those impossible positions which he thinks it proper that you should assume. He would contort your muscles and dislocate your bones like any osteopath. He would burn you with red-hot coals to stop your bleeding, and thrust wires into you to assist your circulation. He would diet you with salt, vinegar, alum, and sometimes, vitriol. Boiling water would be poured on your feet when you seemed ready to faint. It would be his boast that he could keep life within you for two or more weeks longer than would have been possible without his treatment. Would you not have preferred to have been killed at once when you were first captured? What were the crimes you must have committed during your past incarnation to warrant such punishment in this?

The wanton waste of flowers among Western communities is even more appalling than the way they are treated by Eastern Flower-Masters. The number of flowers cut daily to adorn the ballrooms and banquet-tables of Europe and America, to be thrown away on the morrow, must be something enormous; if strung together they might garland a continent. Beside this utter carelessness of life, the guilt of the Flower-Master becomes insignificant. He, at least, respects the economy of nature, selects his victims with careful foresight, and after death does honour to their remains. In the West the display of flowers seems to be a part of the pageantry of wealth,—the fancy of a moment. Whither do they all go, these flowers, when the revelry is over? Nothing is more pitiful than to see a faded flower remorselessly flung upon a dung heap.

Why were the flowers born so beautiful and yet so hapless? Insects can sting, and even the meekest of beasts will fight when brought to bay. The birds whose plumage is sought to deck some bonnet can fly from its pursuer, the furred animal whose coat you covet for your own may hide at your approach. Alas! The only flower known to have wings is the butterfly; all others stand helpless before the destroyer. If they shriek in their death agony their cry never reaches our hardened ears. We are ever brutal to those who love and serve us in silence, but the time may come when, for our cruelty, we shall be deserted by these best friends of ours. Have you not noticed that the wild flowers are becoming scarcer every year? It may be that their wise men have told them to depart till man becomes more human. Perhaps they have migrated to heaven.

Much may be said in favour of him who cultivates plants. The man of the pot is far more humane than he of the scissors. We watch with delight his concern about water and sunshine, his feuds with parasites, his horror of frosts, his anxiety when the buds come slowly, his rapture when the leaves attain their lustre. In the East the art of floriculture is a very ancient one, and the loves of a poet and his favourite plant have often been recorded in story and song. With the development of ceramics during the T'ang and Sung dynasties we hear of wonderful receptacles made to hold plants, not pots, but jewelled palaces. A special attendant was detailed to wait upon each flower and to wash its leaves with soft brushes made of rabbit hair. It has been written* that the peony should

* *P'ing Tzü* by Yuen-chun-liang.

be bathed by a handsome maiden in full costume, that a winter-plum should be watered by a pale, slender monk. In Japan, one of the most popular of the No dances, the Hachinoki, composed during the Ashikaga period, is based upon the story of an impoverished knight, who, on a freezing night, in lack of fuel for a fire, cuts his cherished plants in order to entertain a wandering friar. The friar is in reality no other than Hojo Tokiyori, the Haroun-Al-Raschid of our tales, and the sacrifice is not without its reward. This opera never fails to draw tears from a Tokyo audience even to-day.

Great precautions were taken for the preservation of delicate blossoms. Emperor Hsüan Sung, of the T'ang dynasty, hung tiny golden bells on the branches in his garden to keep off the birds. He it was who went off in the springtime with his court musicians to gladden the flowers with soft music. A quaint tablet, which tradition ascribes to Yoshitsune, the hero of our Arthurian legends,[25] is still extant in one of the Japanese monasteries.* It is a notice put up for the protection of a certain wonderful plum-tree, and appeals to us with the grim humour of a warlike age. After referring to the beauty of the blossoms, the inscription says: "Whoever cuts a single branch of this tree shall forfeit a finger therefor." Would that such laws could be enforced nowadays against those who wantonly destroy flowers and mutilate objects of art!

Yet even in the case of pot flowers we are inclined to suspect the selfishness of man. Why take the plants from their homes and ask them to bloom mid strange surroundings? Is it not like asking the birds to sing and mate cooped up in cages? Who knows but that the orchids feel stifled by the artificial heat in

*Sumadera, near Kobe.

your conservatories and hopelessly long for a glimpse of their own Southern skies?

The ideal lover of flowers is he who visits them in their native haunts, like Tao Yüan Ming,* who sat before a broken bamboo fence in converse with the wild chrysanthemum, or Lin Ho Ching,* losing himself amid mysterious fragrance as he wandered in the twilight among the plum-blossoms of the Western Lake. 'Tis said that Chou Mou Shu* slept in a boat so that his dreams might mingle with those of the lotus. It was this same spirit which moved the Empress Komio, one of our most renowned Nara sovereigns, as she sang: "If I pluck thee, my hand will defile thee, O Flower! Standing in the meadows as thou art, I offer thee to the Buddhas of the past, of the present, of the future."

However, let us not be too sentimental. Let us be less luxurious but more magnificent. Said Lao Tzŭ: "Heaven and earth are pitiless." Said Kobo Daishi: "Flow, flow, flow, flow, the current of life is ever onward. Die, die, die, die, death comes to all." Destruction faces us wherever we turn. Destruction below and above, destruction behind and before. Change is the only Eternal,—why not as welcome Death as Life? They are but counterparts one of the other,—the Night and Day of Brahma. Through the disintegration of the old, re-creation becomes possible. We have worshipped Death, the relentless goddess of mercy, under many different names. It was the shadow of the All-devouring that the Gheburs greeted in the fire. It is the icy purism of the sword-soul before which Shinto-Japan prostrates herself even to-day. The mystic fire consumes our weakness, the sacred sword cleaves the bondage of

---

* All celebrated Chinese poets and philosophers.

desire. From our ashes springs the phoenix of celestial hope, out of the freedom comes a higher realisation of manhood.

Why not destroy flowers if thereby we can evolve new forms ennobling the world idea? We only ask them to join in our sacrifice to the beautiful. We shall atone for the deed by consecrating ourselves to Purity and Simplicity. Thus reasoned the tea-masters when they established the Cult of Flowers.

Anyone acquainted with the ways of our tea- and flower-masters must have noticed the religious veneration with which they regard flowers. They do not cull at random, but carefully select each branch or spray with an eye to the artistic composition they have in mind. They would be ashamed should they chance to cut more than were absolutely necessary. It may be remarked in this connection that they always associate the leaves, if there be any, with the flower, for their object is to present the whole beauty of plant life. In this respect, as in many others, their method differs from that pursued in Western countries. Here we are apt to see only the flower stems, heads, as it were, without body, stuck promiscuously into a vase.

When a tea-master has arranged a flower to his satisfaction he will place it on the tokonoma, the place of honour in a Japanese room. Nothing else will be placed near it which might interfere with its effect, not even a painting, unless there be some special aesthetic reason for the combination. It rests there like an enthroned prince, and the guests or disciples on entering the room will salute it with a profound bow before making their addresses to the host. Drawings from masterpieces are made and published for the edification of amateurs. The amount of literature on the subject is quite voluminous. When the flower fades, the master tenderly consigns it to the river or carefully buries it in the ground. Monuments even are sometimes erected to its memory.

The birth of the Art of Flower-Arrangement seems to be simultaneous with that of Teaism in the fifteenth century. Our legends ascribe the first flower-arrangement to those early Buddhist saints who gathered the flowers strewn by the storm and, in their infinite solicitude for all living things, placed them in vessels of water. It is said that Soami, the great painter and connoisseur of the court of Ashikaga Yoshimasa, was one of the earliest adepts at it. Juko, the tea-master, was one of his pupils, as was also Senno, the founder of the house of Ikenobo, a family as illustrious in the annals of flowers as was that of the Kanos in painting. With the perfecting of the tea-ritual under Rikyu, in the latter part of the sixteenth century, flower-arrangement also attains its full growth. Rikyu and his successors, the celebrated Oda Uraku, Furuta Oribe, Koetsu, Kobori Enshu, and Katagiri Sekishu, vied with each other in forming new combinations.[26] We must remember, however, that the flower worship of the tea-masters formed only a part of their aesthetic ritual, and was not a distinct religion by itself. A flower-arrangement, like the other works of art in the tea-room, was subordinated to the total scheme of decoration. Thus Sekishu ordained that white plum blossoms should not be made use of when snow lay in the garden. "Noisy" flowers were relentlessly banished from the tea-room. A flower-arrangement by a tea-master loses its significance if removed from the place for which it was originally intended, for its lines and proportions have been specially worked out with a view to its surroundings.

The adoration of the flower for its own sake begins with the rise of "Flower-Masters," toward the middle of the seventeenth century. It now becomes independent of the tea-room and knows no law save that that the vase imposes on it. New conceptions and methods of execution now become possible, and many were the principles and schools resulting therefrom. A writer in the middle of the last century said he could count over one hundred different schools of flower-arrangement. Broadly speaking, these divide themselves into two main branches, the Formalistic and the Naturalesque. The Formalistic schools, led by the Ikenobos, aimed at a classic idealism corresponding to that of the Kano academicians. We possess records of arrangements by the early masters of this school which almost reproduce the flower paintings of Sansetsu and Tsunenobu.[27] The Naturalesque school, on the other hand, as its name implies, accepted nature as its model, only imposing such modifications of form as conduced to the expression of artistic unity. Thus we recognise in its works the same impulses which formed the Ukiyoe and Shijo schools of painting.

It would be interesting, had we time, to enter more fully than is now possible into the laws of composition and detail formulated by the various flower-masters of this period, showing, as they would, the fundamental theories which governed Tokugawa decoration. We find them referring to the Leading Principle (Heaven), the Subordinate Principle (Earth), and the Reconciling Principle (Man), and any flower-arrangement which did not embody these principles was considered barren and dead. They also dwelt much on the importance of treating a flower in its three different aspects, the Formal, the Semi-

Formal, and the Informal. The first might be said to represent flowers in the stately costume of the ballroom, the second in the easy elegance of afternoon dress, the third in the charming deshabille of the boudoir.

Our personal sympathies are with the flower-arrangement of the tea-master rather than with that of the flower-master. The former is art in its proper setting and appeals to us on account of its true intimacy with life. We should like to call this school the Natural in contradistinction to the Naturalesque and Formalistic schools. The tea-master deems his duty ended with the selection of the flowers, and leaves them to tell their own story. Entering a tea-room in late winter, you may see a slender spray of wild cherries in combination with a budding camellia; it is an echo of departing winter coupled with the prophecy of spring. Again, if you go into a noon-tea on some irritatingly hot summer day, you may discover in the darkened coolness of the tokonoma a single lily in a hanging vase; dripping with dew, it seems to smile at the foolishness of life.

A solo of flowers is interesting, but in a concerto with painting and sculpture the combination becomes entrancing. Sekishu once placed some water-plants in a flat receptacle to suggest the vegetation of lakes and marshes, and on the wall above he hung a painting by Soami of wild ducks flying in the air. Shoha,[28] another tea-master, combined a poem on the Beauty of Solitude by the Sea with a bronze incense burner in the form of a fisherman's hut and some wild flowers of the beach. One of the guests has recorded that he felt in the whole composition the breath of waning autumn.

Flower stories are endless. We shall recount but

one more. In the sixteenth century the morning-glory was as yet a rare plant with us. Rikyu had an entire garden planted with it, which he cultivated with assiduous care. The fame of his convolvuli reached the ear of the Taikō, and he expressed a desire to see them, in consequence of which Rikyu invited him to a morning tea at his house. On the appointed day the Taikō walked through the garden, but nowhere could he see any vestige of the convolvulus. The ground had been levelled and strewn with fine pebbles and sand. With sullen anger the despot entered the tea-room, but a sight awaited him there which completely restored his humour. On the tokonoma, in a rare bronze of Sung workmanship, lay a single morning-glory—the queen of the whole garden!

In such instances we see the full significance of the Flower Sacrifice. Perhaps the flowers appreciate the full significance of it. They are not cowards, like men. Some flowers glory in death—certainly the Japanese cherry blossoms do, as they freely surrender themselves to the winds. Anyone who has stood before the fragrant avalanche at Yoshino or Arashiyama must have realised this. For a moment they hover like bejewelled clouds and dance above the crystal streams; then, as they sail away on the laughing waters, they seem to say: "Farewell, O Spring! We are on to Eternity."

VII. TEA-MASTERS

In religion the Future is behind us. In art the Present is the Eternal. The tea-masters held that real appreciation of art is only possible to those who make of it a living influence. Thus they sought to regulate their daily life by the high standard of refinement which obtained in the tea-room. In all circumstances serenity of mind should be maintained, and conversation should be so conducted as never to mar the harmony of the surroundings. The cut and colour of the dress, the poise of the body, and the manner of walking could all be made expressions of artistic personality. These were matters not to be lightly ignored, for until one has made himself beautiful he has no right to approach beauty. Thus the tea-master strove to be something more than the artist,—art itself. It was the Zen of aestheticism. Perfection is everywhere if we only choose to recognise it. Rikyu loved to quote an old poem which says: "To those who long only for flowers, fain would I show the full-blown spring which abides in the toiling buds of snow-covered hills."

Manifold indeed have been the contributions of the tea-masters to art. They completely revolutionised the classical architecture and interior decorations and established the new style which we have described in the chapter of the tea-room, a style to whose influence even the palaces and monasteries built after the sixteenth century have all been subject. The many-sided Kobori Enshu has left

61

notable examples of his genius in the Imperial villa of Katsura, the castles of Nagoya and Nijo, and the monastery of Kōhō-an. All the celebrated gardens of Japan were laid out by the tea-masters. Our pottery would probably never have attained its high quality of excellence if the tea-masters had not lent to it their inspiration, the manufacture of the utensils used in the tea-ceremony calling forth the utmost expenditure of ingenuity on the part of our ceramists. The Seven Kilns of Enshu are well known to all students of Japanese pottery. Many of our textile fabrics bear the names of tea-masters who conceived their colour or design. It is impossible, indeed, to find any department of art in which the tea-masters have not left marks of their genius. In painting and lacquer it seems almost superfluous to mention the immense service they have rendered. One of the greatest schools of painting owes its origin to the tea-master Honāmi Koetsu, famed also as a lacquer artist and potter. Beside his works, the splendid creation of his grandson, Kōhō, and of his grand-nephews, Kōrin and Kenzan,[29] almost fall into the shade. The whole Kōrin school, as it is generally designated, is an expression of Teaism. In the broad lines of this school we seem to find the vitality of nature herself.

Great as has been the influence of the tea-masters in the field of art, it is as nothing compared to that which they have exerted on the conduct of life. Not only in the usages of polite society, but also in the arrangement of all our domestic details, do we feel the presence of the tea-masters. Many of our delicate dishes, as well as our way of serving food, are their inventions. They have taught us to dress only in garments of sober colours. They have instructed us in the proper spirit in which to approach flowers.

They have given emphasis to our natural love of simplicity, and shown us the beauty of humility. In fact, through their teachings tea has entered the life of the people.

Those of us who know not the secret of properly regulating our own existence on this tumultuous sea of foolish troubles which we call life are constantly in a state of misery while vainly trying to appear happy and contented. We stagger in the attempt to keep our moral equilibrium, and see forerunners of the tempest in every cloud that floats on the horizon. Yet there is joy and beauty in the roll of the billows as they sweep outward toward eternity. Why not enter into their spirit, or, like Lieh Tsŭ, ride upon the hurricane itself?

He only who has lived with the beautiful can die beautifully. The last moments of the great tea-masters were as full of exquisite refinement as had been their lives. Seeking always to be in harmony with the great rhythm of the universe, they were ever prepared to enter the unknown. The "Last Tea of Rikyu" will stand forth forever as the acme of tragic grandeur.

Long had been the friendship between Rikyu and the Taikō Hideyoshi, and high the estimation in which the great warrior held the tea-master. But the friendship of a despot is ever a dangerous honour. It was an age rife with treachery, and men trusted not even their nearest kin. Rikyu was no servile courtier, and had often dared to differ in argument with his fierce patron. Taking advantage of the coldness which had for some time existed between the Taikō and Rikyu, the enemies of the latter accused him of being implicated in a conspiracy to poison the despot. It was whispered to Hideyoshi that the fatal potion was to be administered to him with a cup of the green beverage prepared by the tea-master. With Hideyoshi suspicion was sufficient ground for instant execution, and there was no appeal from the will of the angry ruler. One privilege alone was granted to the condemned—the honour of dying by his own hand.

On the day destined for his self-immolation, Rikyu invited his chief disciples to a last tea-ceremony. Mournfully at the appointed time the guests met at the portico. As they look into the garden path the trees seem to shudder, and in the rustling of their leaves are heard the whispers of homeless ghosts. Like solemn sentinels before the gates of Hades stand the grey stone lanterns. A wave of rare incense is wafted from the tea-room; it is the summons which bids the guests to enter. One by one they advance and take their places. In the toko-noma hangs a kakemono,—a wonderful writing by an ancient monk dealing with the evanescence of all earthly things. The singing kettle, as it boils over the brazier, sounds like some cicada pouring forth his woes to departing summer. Soon the host enters the room. Each in turn is served with tea, and each in turn silently drains his cup, the host last of all. According to established etiquette, the chief guest now asks permission to examine the tea-equipage. Rikyu places the various articles before them, with the kakemono. After all have expressed admiration of their beauty, Rikyu presents one of them to each of the assembled company as a souvenir. The bowl alone he keeps. "Never again shall this cup, polluted by the lips of misfortune, be used by man." He speaks, and breaks the vessel into fragments.

The ceremony is over; the guests with difficulty restraining their tears, take their last farewell and leave the room. One only, the nearest and dearest, is requested to remain and witness the end. Rikyu then removes his tea-gown and carefully folds it upon the mat, thereby disclosing the immaculate white death robe which it had hitherto concealed. Tenderly he gazes on the shining blade of the fatal dagger, and in exquisite verse thus addresses it:[30]

> Welcome to thee,
> O sword of eternity!
> Through Buddha
> And through Daruma alike
> Thou hast cleft thy way.

With a smile upon his face Rikyu passed forth into the unknown.

AFTERWORD

It seems very probable that Okakura never bothered to read through *The Book of Tea*, either in galley form or in bound copies, for the first edition contains an embarrassing number of misprints and errors. Some of these errors are probably due to the printer, others probably result from faulty memory and hasty writing on Okakura's part. These errors have been perpetuated in all later reprints, although an attempt was made in the Angus and Robertson Australian edition of 1935 to correct and modernize the Japanese spelling.

Where errors have consisted simply of typographical mistakes (as in the misprint Voshimana for the name of the Japanese Shogun Yoshimasa) I have corrected them without comment. Where larger problems have been involved I have used notes, as below, and have not altered Okakura's text: it would be too easy to destroy its flavor and charm.

A further problem has arisen from Okakura's persistent habit of using Japanese versions for Chinese words and proper names. For example, he uses the Japanese name Soshi several times when referring to the Chinese philosopher known to the Chinese and to the West as Chuang Tzŭ. This is unfortunate, for while most readers who have some acquaintance with Oriental thought would recognize the Chinese terms, very few are acquainted with their Japanese counterparts, which are at best parochial, and much of Okakura's point is likely to be lost. For this reason I have inserted accepted Chinese names in the Wade-Giles romanization in brackets after Okakura's terminology.

1 (p. 2). Lao Tzŭ; Chinese philosopher of the sixth century B.C., traditionally an older contemporary of Confucius. The *Tao-te-king*, which next to the Bible is the work most often translated into English, is traditionally ascribed to him, though this attribution is questioned by some modern scholars. His system of thought is mystical, individualistic, empathetic to the universe, and contemplative, as opposed to the social concepts of Confucianism.

2 (p. 2). Sakyamuni; the historical Buddha, Gautama or Siddhartha. The name means "Sage of the Sakyas," the Sakyas being Gautama's clan.

3 (p. 4). Sister Nivedita: Margaret Noble (1867–1911). An Englishwoman who became a convert to Hinduism via the Ramakrishna Order, assuming the name Sister Nivedita. She conducted a school for young Hindu girls, and *The Web of Indian Life*, which presents a highly-colored appreciation of the spiritual values of Hinduism, is based upon her experiences.

4 (p. 6). This paragraph contains several errors. The Arabian traveler in question was Abuzeid el Hazen, cited by Eusebius Renaudot in *Accounts of India and China by Two Mohammedan Travelers Who Went to Those Parts in the Ninth Century*, English translation (London, 1733). I do not see why Okakura should consider this a European record.

The statement about Marco Polo is incorrect. There is no reference to tea in the Yule edition of Marco Polo, although a questionable passage referring to cloves from the highlands of Assam might be a garbled reference to tea.

Giambattista Ramusio (1485–1557) was not a traveler, but a compiler of voyages; the first mention of tea occurs in his *Navigatione et Viaggi* (1559), Volume II. F. Louis Almeida was a missionary who mentioned tea in a letter written in 1565; this letter was printed in a collection of material edited by Giovanni Maffei (printed

"Maffeno" in Okakura's original text) in 1588. Taxeira (printed "Tareira" in Okakura's original text) was a Portuguese who had been at Malacca before 1600.

The exact quotation: "That Excellent, and by all Physitians approved, *China* drink, called by the *Chineans*, *Tcha*, by other Nations *Tay alias Tee*, is sold at the Sultaness-Head, a *Cophee-house* in Sweetings Rents, by the Royal Exchange, *London*." This, the first advertisement for tea, appeared in the *Mercurius Politicus* for September 30, 1658. It is reproduced in facsimile in William H. Ukers' definitive *All About Tea* (Trade Journal Company; New York, 1935), Volume I, page 42. (The footnote in other editions referring the *Mercurius Politicus* for 1656 to the Russian diffusion of tea is in error.)

5 (p. 6). *Journal of an Eight Days Journey from Portsmouth to Kingston-upon-Thames, to which is added an Essay on Tea, considered as Pernicious to Health, obstructing Industry and Impoverishing the Nation* (London, 1756). The *Essay on Tea* has been reprinted separately.

6 (p. 7). This quotation is taken from Samuel Johnson's review of Hanway's book. It varies slightly from text to text. The version from Johnson's collected works states that Hanway can not expect impartiality from "a hardened and shameless tea-drinker, who has for many years diluted his meals with only the infusion of this fascinating plant; whose kettle has scarcely time to cool; who with tea amuses the evening, with tea solaces the midnight, and with tea welcomes the morning." Johnson, as is well-known, thought nothing of drinking thirty or forty cups of tea a day.

7 (p. 8). Niuka [Nü Wa]. Okakura's poetic myth differs quite a bit from the versions usually found in Chinese sources. Nü K'ua Shih, or Nü Wa, was one of the early mythical rulers of China, the sister, consort, and successor to the first of the Three Emperors, Fu Hsi.

She reigned by the supernatural power of wood, or the principle of construction; one of her vassals, K'ung K'ung, rebelled and tried to overthrow her reign by the power of water, or dissolution. K'ung K'ung was beaten by General Chu Yung, who later became the god of fire. K'ung K'ung struck his head against the Imperfect Mountain, shattered it, and fractured the supports that held up the heavens. Nü K'ua thereupon melted the five precious metals in her cauldron and repaired the heavens; as new supports for the four corners, she placed the feet of the cosmic tortoise. More detailed English versions of this etiological myth can be found in *The Mythology of All Races*, Volume VIII, *Chinese*, by John C. Ferguson (Boston, 1937) and *Myths and Legends of China*, by E. T. C. Werner (London, 1922).

8 (p. 9). The great Avatar. Revelation, according to Buddhism, is a continuous process, and another Buddha is due to be born on Earth in the not too distant future. Maitreya by name (Miroku in Japanese), he will be the embodiment of mercy, and will carry on the work of salvation begun by previous Buddhas.

9 (p. 10). Sesson; Japanese painter (1485–1570). Renowned for misty, subdued landscapes; in the school of Sesshiu.

10 (p. 10). Lichihlai [Li Chi Lai]. This seems to be an error in Okakura's text. Hiroshi Muraoka, the editor of the Japanese edition of *The Book of Tea* (Tokyo, 1938), has suggested that this is an error for Li Chi Chin. In Japanese pronunciation the last character would be read "kei," which written in bad handwriting in English might be misread as "lai." Muraoka adds, however, that the quotation is not to be found in Li Chi Chin.

11 (p. 11). The Chinese dynasties:

Shang	Eighteenth century B. C. – twelfth century B. C.
Chou	Twelfth century B. C.–249 B. C.
Ch'in	246 B. C.–207 B. C.
Han	206 B. C.–220 A.D.

Interim of the Three Kingdoms

Sui   589 A. D.–618 A. D.
T'ang   618 A. D.–906 A. D.

Interim of the Five Dynasties

Sung   960 A. D.–1279 A. D.
Mongol (Yüan)   1280 A. D.–1368 A. D.
Ming   1368 A. D.–1644 A. D.
Manchu (Ch'ing)   1644 A. D.–1911 A. D.

12 (p. 12). Tea preparation. From the *Kuang Ya* by Chang I, fifth century A. D.: "To make tea as a drink, bake the cake until reddish in color, pound it into tiny pieces, put them in a chinaware pot, pour boiling water over them, and add onion, ginger, and orange." Quoted from Ukers' *All about Tea* (see Note 4).

13 (p. 12). Lu Wu, or Lu Yü (died 804 A. D.); author of the first known book about tea. A detailed biography of Lu Wu and an extended summary of the *Ch'a Ching*, with sections in translation, are to be found in Ukers' *All About Tea* (see Note 4).

14 (p. 14). Horaisan. The Chinese form is P'eng-lai-shan. Mythical islands in the Eastern sea, commonly associated with immortality. These islands play an important part in Chinese and Japanese literary folklore, especially in the Taoist alchemical tradition, where the elixir of life was sought. According to Chinese belief, a mushroom conferring immortality was to be found there, while the Japanese believed that the tree of life grew on the central island. During the Chinese middle ages many individuals and expeditions are said to have sailed eastward looking for these islands.

15 (p. 16). Bodhidharma; in Japanese often called Daruma. A semi-legendary figure, Bodhidharma is said to have brought Mahayana Buddhism from India to China, arriving in Canton via the sea route around 520

A. D. He is the first Zen patriarch, and is associated with remarkable abilities in yogic meditation. According to one legend his legs atrophied from disuse and dropped off, for which reason his images are usually legless, and are profanely called snowmen. According to another legend, when he found that fatigue caused his eyelids to drop, interfering with his meditation, he cut off his lids, which turned into tea leaves.

16 (p. 17). Saicho; better known by his later name, Dengyo Daishi. He had been sent to China by the Emperor of Japan to gather cultural information. He is regarded as having introduced the Tendai sect of Buddhism to Japan.

17 (p. 19). Kwanyin [Yin Hsi]. This person is not to be confused with the Chinese Buddhist deity Kwanyin, the merciful madonna-like figure so often portrayed in Chinese and Japanese art. (The normal Japanese form for the bodhisattva is Kwannon or Kannon.) According to the traditional biography of Lao Tzŭ, at an advanced age Lao Tzŭ saw that the kingdom of Chou where he lived was about to collapse, and recognized that his teachings were disregarded. Mounting a buffalo he rode to the west, out of China, and disappeared. Upon passing through the Han Pass in modern Honan, he was stopped by the warder of the gate, Yin Hsi, also known as Kwan Yin, who begged him to stop for a time. Yin Hsi, who was himself a renowned sage, had been waiting by a grass hut for years, in the expectation that an Immortal would go through the pass. Yin Hsi persuaded Lao Tzŭ to write his teachings down, and the result was the manuscript of the *Tao-te-king,* or the great book of the Taoists.

18 (p. 21). Southern vs. Northern Chinese cultural personalities. However true Okakura's statement may have been for later times, it is incorrect to consider Lao Tzŭ and the early Taoists as Southerners, or to claim that their ideas are of Southern origin. Chinese

culture at the time of Confucius was still concentrated in the North, there was a tremendous variety of religious and philosophical speculation at this crucial time in China, and Lao Tzŭ was practically a neighbor of Confucius's.

19 (p. 23). Lieh Tzŭ; Taoist philosopher traditionally assigned to the fourth pre-Christian century. "There was also Lieh Tzŭ, who let himself be carried by the wind with the greatest indifference. He did not return for fifteen days. He was completely free from all worldly endeavor for fortune." Translated from *Dschuang Dsi, Das Wahre Buch vom Südlichen Blütenland*, Richard Wilhelm, translator (Jena, 1923).

20 (p. 28). A cult of relics has long been a part of Buddhism, for after the death of Gautama fragments from his cremation (including the burned coals) were enshrined. According to some Buddhist groups, the attainment of Buddhahood (becoming a bodhisattva) is marked by physiological signs, including some features that will persist after death. A chain of calcified glands around the neck, for example, is known as Buddha's necklace, and individual beads may be sought after for magical purposes. Okakura's note to shah-li ("Shali") reads: "The precious jewels formed in the bodies of Buddhas after cremation." I believe that this should read "found" rather than "formed."

21 (p. 31). Sukiya. Because of its large vocabulary of Chinese origin, Japanese has remarkable abilities for creating puns and deliberate ambiguities. The true term for a tea-pavilion would be "sukiya," which is practically a direct equivalent of our English "pleasure-house." But there are several different Japanese words "suki," with very different meanings; each has its own Chinese character, since the characters primarily convey meaning rather than sound:

好 家	sukiya pleasure-house, place of pleasure
空 家	sukiya place of emptiness, from "suku": to be empty
數 寄 家	sukiya place of tastefulness and décor
數 奇 家	sukiya place of varied fortunes

The last combination, which Okakura translates as "the Unsymmetrical," in modern idiom is really equivalent to "ups and downs, a checkered career, a colorful life," with a slight pejorative connotation.

These figures of speech are deliberate, of course, but where there is an ambiguity in Japanese (and even more in Chinese) it is not infrequent for a speaker to sketch rapidly with his finger on his palm the character that conveys the meaning that he intends.

22 (p. 31). Hideyoshi (1536–1598); the de facto ruler of Japan from 1582 to 1598, often called the Napoleon of Japan. During this period of Japanese history, the Emperor was a cultic figurehead who had only ceremonial duties and no real power; the shogun, who had supplanted the Emperor, became a figurehead too, with his office a hereditary position in the Minamoto family; the real power was concentrated in the hands of feudal warlords and military dictators. Hideyoshi, a peasant by origin, became a lieutenant to the clan general Nobunaga, and upon Nobunaga's death became dictator of Japan, eventually receiving the title "Taikō." Under Hideyoshi's rule, Japan, which had broken down into semi-independent feudatories, was unified; a strong central government was established, European intrigues were halted, and Japan undertook an only partly successful invasion of China and Korea. Hideyoshi was a brilliant general and administrator, but was irascible, suspicious, and ruthless.

23 (p. 33). Kasyapa and Ananda; two followers of

Gautama, the historical Buddha. Upon the death of Gautama, Kasyapa became leader of the group, and was later followed by Ananda, the Buddha's favorite disciple. The Zen historians state that Kasyapa and Ananda were aware of a secret tradition, the Zen, which they passed on without revealing it to the world at large. Other Buddhist sects do not share this point of view.

24 (p. 34). Manjusri; a bodhisattva, the personification of wisdom and intellect, especially revered in China and Japan.

25 (p. 54). Yoshitsune. Okakura's comparison of Yoshitsune with King Arthur is somewhat misleading, except that both heroes have provided limitless resources to folk narrators, poets, dramatists and novelists. Yoshitsune (1159–1189) was a historical person whose heroism and tragic fate have always aroused sympathy among the Japanese. During the War of the Gempei, when the rival clans of Taira and Minamoto were fighting for control of Japan, it was due largely to Yoshitsune's brilliance that the Taira were beaten on land and sea. His older brother, Yoritomo, the head of the clan, became shogun but, jealous of Yoshitsune's popularity and ability, exiled him from the court. He was eventually pursued into the wastes of Northern Japan by assassins sent by Yoritomo, and probably committed suicide.

Yoshitsune is the chivalric hero par excellence of medieval Japan, and the episodes of his life combine something of the personalities and auras of Robin Hood, Bayard, and Sir Galahad. Orphaned by an early clan skirmish, he was reared at a Buddhist temple, but spent his evenings secretly in military practice. Before starting his work as a knight errant and general, he acquired his equally famous lieutenant, the giant monk Benkei, after a staff and sword battle upon a bridge, reminiscent of Robin Hood's encounter with Little John. According to folklore he won many combats and subdued many ogres before achieving his destiny as a Minamoto general.

26 (p. 57). Tea-masters and their dates: Juko, 1422–1502; Rikyu, 1521–1591; Oda Uraku, 1552–1621; Furuta Oribe, 1543–1615; Koetsu, 1568–1637; Kobori Enshu, 1579–1647; Katagiri Sekishu, 1605–1673. (See also Notes 27–29.)

27 (p. 58). Sansetsu, 1589–1651; Tsunenobu, 1636–1713.

28 (p. 59). Shoha, 1524–1600.

29 (p. 62). Kōhō, 1601–1682; Kōrin, 1661–1716; Kenzan, 1663–1743.

30 (p. 65). Rikyu's farewell really consisted of a Japanese poem and a Chinese poem, which Okakura seems to have blended freely into a single stanza. Daisetz Suzuki, in his *Zen and Japanese Culture* (New York, 1959), page 319, has given literal translations of both poems.